METRO BOOKS
New York

Sterling Publishing Co., Inc.
New York, NY

METRO BOOKS and the distinctive Metro Books logo
are registered trademarks of Sterling Publishing Co., Inc.

ISBN 978-1-4351-6929-6

For information about custom editions, special sales, and premium and corporate
purchases, please contact Sterling Special Sales at 800-805-5489 or
specialsales@sterlingpublishing.com.

Manufactured in Singapore

4 6 8 10 9 7 5 3

sterlingpublishing.com

Design: JC Lanaway
Photo credits: see page 224

UNSOLVED ENIGMAS

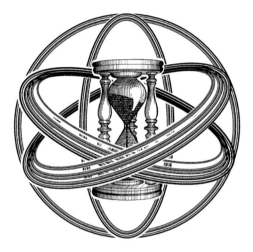

INCREDIBLE EVENTS THAT HAVE PUZZLED THE GREATEST MINDS

SAM PILGER & LEO MOYNIHAN

METRO BOOKS
New York

CONTENTS

INTRODUCTION

Modern life seems so certain. Technology allows us to find instantaneous answers to our questions, with social media on hand to crowd-source opinions, satellite navigation systems in our cars to tell us which way to turn, and the World Wide Web to answer the most complex of questions to even the oldest of queries. In this modern world, there is black and there is white—and woe betide any of us who still prefer to wallow in the gray. Yet it is in that gray that our curiosity can be best nurtured; it is there that our desire to question is satisfied; and it is there that questions can remain unanswered.

While humankind has prospered by its never-ending hunger for knowledge and improvement, there are aspects of our lives and our past that perhaps are best never fully known. Enigmas and mysteries are fundamental to our lives. Yes, we want to solve every question put in front of us, but the unexplained remains vital to human growth, and this book celebrates those enigmatic events, people, sightings, and hauntings that frankly are better off concluded with a question mark. Within these pages, we look at the unpredictable; at events and persons through time that were seemingly unable to be controlled. We go back to Ancient Egypt and ask why a mummy was found screaming. We risk British treason laws by questioning whether William Shakespeare wrote all of his plays alone.

There are disappearances that continue to baffle. Ships veering off-course into unknown realms have long intrigued and are covered here with the *Carroll A. Deering*, but we also look at more. Why was the racehorse Shergar taken and what was his fate, and what of the rock band Manic Street Preachers and the fate of their one-time guitarist Richey Edwards?

The supernatural is of course covered— ghosts and possession will always prick the darker side of human curiosity. Was the famous Enfield Haunting—or the strange Faces of Bélmez that appeared on the walls of a modest Spanish home—just a hoax or something much more sinister?

Above: The disappearance of world-famous, Derby-winning Shergar has fascinated people since 1983—who was responsible and what happened to this iconic racehorse?

Creatures, like the supernatural, appeal to something carnal within us, something intrinsically linked to our childhoods. Names such as the Chupacabra and the Altamaha-ha, both covered within these pages, go some way to satiating that carnal fascination.

And then there are people. By no means supernatural or of another world but equally as enigmatic. Who was the Isdal Woman, and why did the lady in the Babushka scarf, present at the death of John F. Kennedy, vanish? Again, these cases—and more—are looked at in detail.

If you are looking for answers, you are in the wrong place: this is a book that celebrates the desire for mystery, a yearning for the unanswered and the unsolved. This is a book that allows you to wallow in the gray.

HISTORICAL ENIGMAS

A mystery of any sort is a thing of intrigue. Add to that a sense of historic realism and you have something even more perplexing. Sightings of weird and fabled creatures, talk of ghostly goings on, and the discovery of unexplained and abandoned places are all fascinating, and prick the curiosity in even the most skeptical of minds. There is something about enigmatic moments from history that puts our imagination into overdrive.

Mysteries surrounding historical icons such as William Shakespeare and Adolf Hitler will always resonate with the public, and in this chapter we challenge long-held perceptions about their lives and, in the case of Hitler, their deaths. Did Shakespeare write his astonishing array of plays, poems, and sonnets alone; and did Hitler, with the Allies closing in on him, really commit suicide?

We look closely at historical characters and events that continue to have us on the edge of our seats. Take the assassination of Robert Kennedy; for so long overlooked in preference to the mystery surrounding his brother's death, but a case that, despite the sentencing of his supposed killer, still requires further reading and questioning to even attempt to reveal the depth of the mystery.

Left: Why, and how, did people dance themselves to death in sixteenth-century Europe?

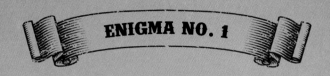

WHAT WAS THE CAUSE OF THE DANCING PLAGUE?

Date: July 1518
Location: Strasbourg, France

In medieval France hundreds of people were suddenly gripped by an irresistible urge to dance, and could not stop for several weeks.

One morning in July 1518, a woman called Frau Troffea left her house in a narrow backstreet of Strasbourg, in what is now northeastern France, and unexpectedly found herself beginning to dance. She danced for the rest of the day before collapsing that evening covered in sweat, and after only a couple of hours' sleep, woke and began to dance all over again until she was utterly exhausted and her shoes were full of blood.

Troffea would remain there, dancing for between four and six days, until she was eventually taken to a shrine to seek help for her condition. She had already attracted another 34 villagers to join her and within a month there were about 400 people who remained in the same place, jumping and jerking around as they performed a strange dance together. The mention of dancing suggests these people were enjoying themselves, but that was never the case. Many were in deep distress; they were in pain, begging for help. It was not their choice to dance—they did so involuntarily, against their will. The dancers wore haunted expressions on their faces, and before long some would collapse from exhaustion, strokes, and heart attacks. There are reports that at the height of the outbreak as many as 15 people a day died through this uncontrollable dancing.

At the time, the local authorities believed the only cure to this outbreak was to continue dancing, and so, incredibly, they actively encouraged the people to do it all day and night. They opened the center of the town to the dancers, including two guildhalls and a grain market, and even constructed a stage in the center of the city for villagers to dance. They also employed professional dancers to dance alongside them and a band to play music. Rather than quell the outbreak, this encouraged it, and even more people joined the dancing throngs.

Below: Told to carry on dancing, in the hope the "disease" would run its course, people were soon dying from the over-exertion.

DANCING SWEEPS THE CONTINENT

The Strasbourg incident has become the most famous case of mass involuntary dancing, but it certainly wasn't the first, as it had occurred several times before in Western Europe. One of the first reports was as far back as 1021, in the German town of Kölbigk, when, on Christmas Eve, 18 people surrounded a church and began to dance. The priest asked them to stop, but they refused and continued to dance in a ring, all of them holding hands and jumping up and down together. In his fury, the priest cursed them to dance for another year, and they did not stop until Christmas 1022, when they collapsed with exhaustion and fell into a sleep, from which some never woke.

Above: Could it be that the dancing victims were hysterical from ingesting ergot fungus, seen here growing on an ear of barley?

There would be further reports of incidents of mass involuntary dancing, including in Erfurt in central Germany in 1247, and then in 1278 in Maastricht in the Netherlands, when 200 people danced on a bridge for so long it collapsed and they all drowned in the Moselle River. During 1374, there were reports that this compulsion to dance swept across western Germany, the Netherlands, Belgium, France, and England. On June 23 of that year, the town of Aachen in Germany witnessed a large group of people gripped by the need to dance.

In the early part of the fifteenth century, a monk was reported to have danced to death in Schaffhausen, Switzerland; a group of women in Zurich were unable to stop themselves dancing in public for many days; and in the German city of Trier a large group of people danced and jumped for over six months before many died of their injuries, including broken bones.

In Strasbourg, and in these other incidents, just what had caused these people to dance for so long against their will, some for so long that it killed them? At first, it was believed the dancers might be possessed by the devil or suffering from an affliction called "hot blood," where victims overheat and cannot control themselves. A popular theory at the time, which has persisted to the present day, is that the dancers were all suffering from a strong form of food poisoning after eating ergot fungus, a psychotropic mold that grows on the stalks of rye and, in a similar way to the drug LSD, can cause hallucinations and spasms. Other areas of medieval Europe suffered with epidemics of what was called "ergotism," but academics have dismissed it as a cause in Strasbourg because if the dancers had been infected with it, they simply would not have had the energy to dance for so long.

— ALTERNATIVE —
THEORIES

Professor John Waller believes the dancing plague was fueled by a phenomenon known as "mass psychogenic illness," a form of mass hysteria brought on by a group of people suffering from stress. "My explanation rests on the fact that the dancers were in a trance state; otherwise they would have been unable to dance for such lengths of time," Waller has said. "We know that the trance state is more likely to occur in people who are under extreme psychological distress."

The residents of Strasbourg were under a great deal of distress at this time, after suffering a poor harvest and a sharp rise in grain prices, which meant some were starving. Many had also seen their friends and neighbors die from malnutrition. At the same time, there had been outbreaks of several diseases that were also killing people, including syphilis, leprosy, smallpox, and a new one called "the English sweat." People were also gripped by a fear that they could be cursed by Saint Vitus, who they believed had the power to control their minds and force them to dance. This fear increased the likelihood they would enter a trance and succumb to the fears they were trying to resist.

Below: Was Saint Vitus responsible for the dancing curse? Here Vitus is depicted in a cauldron, as was popular during the Middle Ages, to represent his torture after conversion to Christianity.

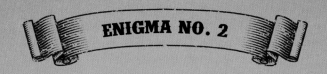
DID WILLIAM SHAKESPEARE WRITE HIS OWN PLAYS?

Date: 1589–1614
Location: England

Shakespeare's complete works are still regarded as the greatest contribution to the English language, but are they really all his own work? Some say not...

In England, questioning the legitimacy of William Shakespeare's work is tantamount to high treason. There are plenty of people, though, who believe that the complete works of the Bard are not in fact the work of one man. There are those who are adamant that William Shakespeare did not work alone.

William Shakespeare was born in Stratford-upon-Avon in 1564. The son of a glove-maker, the young man took up acting before writing 38 plays, 154 sonnets, and 5 poems, all of which continue to be performed, studied, revered, and adapted 400 years after his death. However, and this is where things get controversial, did Shakespeare write this body of work without assistance?

THE DOUBTS BEGIN

In 1781 a literary scholar named James Wilmot set out to write a comprehensive biography of Shakespeare and in doing so, started a school of thought known as the Anti-Stratfordian Theory. Wilmot had visited Stratford-upon-Avon and the surrounding areas, taking in the homes probably visited by his subject, the libraries of the region, and seeking out any correspondence sent or received by Shakespeare.

Wilmot was astonished to discover no evidence that Shakespeare ever wrote a book or a letter. He found no books containing Shakespeare's handwriting, no scribbled musings within old bibles, no signed letters. The biographer deduced that a man who it was claimed wrote so prolifically and with so much passion, must surely also be one who had left a trail of words. As he could not find such a trail, Wilmot started to believe that the works of the Bard had not been written by Shakespeare at all.

Above: The historic home of Mary Arden, mother of William Shakespeare, is now iconic, but some argue that Shakespeare's humble origins cast doubt over his ability to write such plays.

Above: Was Francis Bacon better placed in society to have been able to write the body of work attributed to Shakespeare?

Such was the love for Shakespeare, even in the early nineteenth century, that Wilmot would not go public with his findings or his conspiracy theories, but those who have shared his mistrust of Shakespeare's credentials believe that in 1805, his friend the lecturer James Corton Powell did. Lectures were apparently discovered in 1931 that had been given by Powell and argued forcibly for the idea that it was not Shakespeare who wrote these great plays, but someone of a far higher standing within English society.

TO BELIEVE OR NOT TO BELIEVE

The Anti-Stratfordian Theory grew more fashionable throughout the nineteenth century. In 1857, Delia Bacon wrote a book arguing that it was Francis Bacon, the Elizabethan author and philosopher, who in fact had written the plays and sonnets. Delia Bacon was not related to Francis, but her book soon garnered much attention. The American novelist Nathaniel Hawthorne wrote the foreword to it, and when Mark Twain read it years later, he, for one, was convinced: "So far as anybody actually knows and can prove, Shakespeare of Stratford-on-Avon never wrote a play in his life," he said in 1909.

Since Twain, many modern commentators have questioned the long-held assumption that one man was responsible for this magnificent body of work. The actor and director Orson Welles, himself a fine performer of Shakespearian prose, refused to conform to the idea that just one man was responsible for the plays he so loved. The civil rights activist Malcolm X became intrigued by the argument, even writing in his autobiography about the "Shakespeare dilemma," wondering, "If Shakespeare existed, he was then the top poet around," so why hadn't Shakespeare been involved in the writing of the King James Bible? "If he existed, why didn't King James use him?" Charlie Chaplin was also an advocate for the Anti-Stratfordian Theory, saying in 1964, "I am not concerned with who wrote the works of Shakespeare … but I can hardly think it was the Stratford boy. Whoever wrote them had an aristocratic attitude."

It is a popular argument. Shakespeare was a man born into a fairly modest background, and many scholars state that a man of his limited education would not have had a grasp of languages, the classics, history, or politics, while a man of the nobility, or so-called higher standing, would. Then there is the sheer body of work. The vast number of plays and sonnets and poems, it is argued by "non-believers," is far too great to belong to just one man. Add that to the fact that there is very little in the way of actual documentation linking a William Shakespeare of Stratford-upon-Avon to the complete works that the world knows and loves, and the argument becomes an interesting one.

Right: Many have studied the language used in Shakespeare's work and argue that the style is far too varied to be the work of one man, pointing to the notion that the plays were written by a number of authors.

THE BARD'S BACKERS

Shakespeare enthusiasts scoff at the argument. In fact, they argue that Shakespeare did receive a high level of education and was well taught when it came to the classics, Latin grammar, and history. They also point to the fact that the vast majority of his 38 plays had his name on their original title pages. Then there are the deeds to the Globe Theatre in London, the venue at which many of Shakespeare's plays were first performed; there is documentation that proves that the William Shakespeare named on them is the same man baptized in Stratford-upon-Avon in 1564.

It seems likely that a William Shakespeare was involved with the writing of these wonderful plays, but it is argued that Elizabethan drama was very much a collaboration, that while one man's genius was a driving force, his body of work owes much to others, and that, like a Hollywood movie, a finished script that is attributed to one screenwriter will actually have been looked at and added to by many different minds. So, whisper it quietly in England, but the complete works of William Shakespeare might indeed not belong to one man alone.

Below: The deeds of the Globe Theatre support the claim that Shakespeare wrote his own work.

— ALTERNATIVE —
THEORIES

The first common theory regarding the true identity of the author of Shakespeare's work pointed at Francis Bacon. Many thought that a man of Bacon's standing and intellect paid William Shakespeare, a mere actor, to put his name to this work, protecting Bacon's anonymity. Others think it was actually Edward de Vere, Earl of Oxford, a favorite within the court of Elizabeth I (until he impregnated one of her maids of honor) and known to be a fine playwright and poet. The queen herself had received an extensive humanist education from her father, Henry VIII, and was known to be a keen scholar, one with a fine grasp for

Above: Some even suggest that Elizabeth I herself was the actual author of Shakespeare's work.

politics, history, languages, rhetoric, and the classics. Of course, being the monarch and a female, putting her own name to a body of work would have been impossible. The theory falls down, though, as there were plays written after the queen's death in 1603, but still, some do believe she was involved in the earlier work. Many also point to Christopher Marlowe, and Thomas Middleton, contemporaries of Shakespeare and widely considered to have collaborated with him on many of his plays.

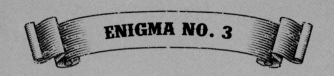

HAS ANYONE BROKEN THE CODE OF THE SHUGBOROUGH INSCRIPTION?

Date: 1748–Present day
Location: Shugborough Hall, Staffordshire, England

In the corner of a quiet garden of an English manor house stands a monument with a code that has baffled all those who have attempted to solve it for nearly three centuries.

In the grounds of the seventeenth-century Shugborough Hall in Staffordshire stands a monument made of stone and marble, known as the Shepherd's Monument. Sculpted by Peter Scheemakers, the monument was built some time between 1748 and 1758 by the Anson family, who owned Shugborough Hall.

It was Thomas Anson, the eldest son of the family and a member of parliament, who conceived and commissioned the monument, which was paid for by his younger brother, Admiral George Anson. In 1740 Anson had commanded a fleet of seven ships on a journey around the world, and in June 1743 he had captured the Spanish ship *Nuestra Señora de Covadonga*, which was laden with gold and jewels. His share of this treasure would help pay for renovations for Shugborough Hall and the building of the monument.

The monument features a replica of *The Arcadian Shepherds*, a renowned painting by Nicolas Poussin, who was a classical French artist in the seventeenth century. The carving of the original painting, which hangs in the Louvre gallery in Paris, depicts a woman and three shepherds around a tomb, upon which are carved the words, "*Et in arcadia ego*" (Latin for "I am also in Arcadia").

Above: Admiral George Anson, hailed as one of Britain's greatest admirals, funded the Shugborough monument.

Above the Arcadian Shepherds are two stone heads: Pan, the Greek god of the wild and of shepherds; the other, a man with a smirk on his face. Below this scene, 10 mysterious letters have been carved into the monument: a "D" and an "M," and then in between them: O U O S V A V V, but no one has ever been able to explain why. It is not known who carved these letters into the monument, or indeed when it happened, for documents have shown that they may have been added in the following century.

CRACKING THE CODE

In the years since, a host of professional codebreakers, including the team from Bletchley Park who solved the Enigma code during World War II, as well as such figures as Charles Darwin and Charles Dickens, have attempted to provide an answer, without any success. Today, it remains one of the great unsolved codes.

At first it was assumed that the "D" and the "M" in the carving stood for *Dis Manibus*, which means "dedicated to the shades," which is often found on Roman tombs; this could be the case, but this monument is not Roman. Could the mysterious letters

Above: The Shepherd's Monument was designed by Thomas Wright and takes its name from the painting it is based on, *The Arcadian Shepherds*.

in the monument be a tribute to Admiral George Anson's wife, Lady Elizabeth Yorke, after her death? In 1951 it was suggested that the letters stood for a Latin phrase, *Optimae uxoris optimae sororis viduus amantissimus vovit virtutibus*, which translates as "Best wife, best sister, widower most loving vows virtuously." In 2004 Sheila Lawn, a member of the Bletchley Park team from the war, endorsed this finding. "I believe in the simple approach, and this appears to be an elegant solution," she said.

The historian A. J. Morton believes the letters were carved into the monument in the century after it was originally built by George Adams, the nephew of Thomas Anson, and his wife Mary Vernon-Venables, who were residents of Shugborough Hall in the nineteenth century. Morton discovered that Adams's wife was the daughter of the 1st Baron Vernon and sister of Edward Vernon-Harcourt, an Archbishop of York. He believes the inscription stands for *Orgreave United with Overley and Shugborough, Viscount Anson Venables Vernon.*

"It is very likely that 'M'ary 'V'enables-'V'ernon of 'S'udbury Hall, the Baron 'V'ernon of 'D'erbyshire, the honorable Edward 'V'ernon-Harcourt, and the 1st 'V'iscount 'A'nson of 'O'rgreave (a hamlet 'U'nited with 'O'verley) and 'S'hugborough were somehow involved in the creation of the original 'Shugborough Code' … I've tried convincing myself that I'm wrong, but I can't see any way out. While I'm pleased to have solved it, I do worry that I've destroyed something magical," Morton said.

In 2014, Keith Massey, a linguist from the National Security Agency in the USA, came forward to say he had cracked the code, and the initials were in Latin and stood for *Oro ut omnes sequantur Viam ad Veram Vitam*: "I pray that all may follow the Way to True Life."

Above: Can you crack the code, and be one of the half-dozen codebreakers who claim every week to have done just that?

"I believe I've solved the mystery," Massey announced. "I believe my proposal provides a sensible and credible interpretation to this long-standing mystery. My solution provides a straightforward and grammatical sentence, all parts of which are attested in tomb inscriptions and texts predating or contemporary with the creation of the Shugborough Inscription."

IT'S ALL CONJECTURE

There has been a raft of other suggestions, including that the letters are not Latin or English but Norwegian, and some say they are not letters at all but numbers. Another Bletchley codebreaker, Oliver Lawn, the husband of Sheila, is not convinced the code will ever be broken, for there is simply not enough to go on: "For any code, you need a minimum amount of encoded material, very much larger than 10 letters," he said in 2004. "No code of 10 letters is possible to break definitively, so to break the Shugborough code, you have to take into account the circumstances and history."

In 2011 a spokesman for Shugborough Hall said they had reports of around five or six people each week claiming to have solved the code.

Right: Members of the team from Bletchley Park, who solved the Enigma code during World War II (using the Enigma Machine, right), have tried to crack the Shugborough code.

— ALTERNATIVE —
THEORIES

In recent years, the owners of Shugborough Hall have been keen to suggest that the inscription can be linked to the Knights Templar and the search for the Holy Grail. It is believed that some members of the Anson family belonged to a secret society called the Priory of Sion, thought to be the successor to the medieval Knights Templar. The Knights, apparently, knew the whereabouts of the Holy Grail, the cup Christ used at the Last Supper. An American, who wished to remain anonymous, used a series of grids to unlock the code, to reveal the message "Jesus H Defy," as he believed the "H" to be *chi*, the Greek letter used for the Messiah. And so here on the monument was a code from the Templars declaring that Jesus was not divine, and just another prophet. It was also rumored that Nicolas Poussin was a grandmaster of the Knights Templar, and so the use of his painting in the carving was another clue to back up this theory.

Above: Does the key to the code lie with the Knights Templar, who famously believed that Jesus Christ was not the son of God?

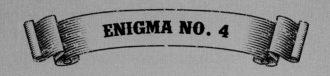

WHY IS THE SCREAMING MUMMY SCREAMING?

Date: 1881–Present day
Location: Deir el-Bahari, Egypt

A nineteenth-century archaeological dig discovered a mummy whose pained face and quick burial suggested foul play.

In 1881, 300 miles (480 kilometers) south of Cairo in Deir el-Bahari, an archaeological dig is well underway. At the end of a 45-foot (14-meter) vertical shaft, 40 Egyptian mummies are discovered. It's an extraordinary find. Past rulers and royalty are disturbed from their slumber of 3,000 years. Among them is an unidentified mummy, at first ignored.

The fact that the body was not identified would soon prick the curiosity of those who made the famous discovery. Experts believed that at the end of the Ramesside period, tomb robbing had become such a serious problem that the high priests began to remove pharaohs from their places of rest to less grandiose sites. Secreted away from prying hands, the mummies were stripped of their most valuable belongings. However, in Ancient Egypt, the most precious asset to a dead man was his identity. Having their name buried with them assured the dead a place in heaven.

ON CLOSE INSPECTION

The body, when closely inspected, had not been preserved like those with whom he had for so long shared a tomb. His arms had been bound in leather; his internal organs and brain were intact (they were usually removed); the act of embalming the body had been done very quickly—no embalming fluids were used, just quicklime, meaning mummification would occur naturally; and he was seemingly quickly put into a cedar box, the interior of which had been crudely hacked in order to widen it. This was no royal burial. Perhaps most tellingly, the body was wrapped, rather than in the customary linen, in sheepskin, indicating that this was an "unclean" body, one not worthy of the afterlife afforded to the most beloved of rulers.

And then there was the expression on the man's face. When the face was uncovered, archaeologists found the facial muscles strained and the mouth agape, contorted as if the man had died screaming. It was unclear whether the man had died in agony, or if the body had been manipulated to give it this terrified expression, but from then on, "Unknown Man E" was known as the Screaming Mummy.

A DELIBERATE ACT

At first, those examining the body presumed their find was an Egyptian who had passed away while serving a governor who traveled abroad within Egypt's vast empire, and that the nature of his burial was due merely to its having been carried out by novices, unaccustomed to Egypt's usual customs. This theory explained why the body was draped in sheepskin, a cloth widely used in burials in other parts of the world. It would also account for why the body was dried out using quicklime.

Below: In 1886, five years after the discovery, the body originally named, simply, "Unknown Man E," was at last afforded a closer look.

That theory was soon discredited due to the fact that the body had been laid to rest in such regal company. Also, the lack of identification, which seemed so intentional, pointed to the idea that this was a purposeful act and that whoever had been involved had hoped to ensure that he would not enter into the afterlife.

Experts were baffled: mummies were never discovered with such pained expressions. Early theories suggested that the man had been poisoned. "We'd never seen a mummy like this, suffering," said Dr. Hawass, a former Minister of Antiquities in Egypt. "It's not normal, and tells us something happened, but we did not know exactly what."

Other theories leaned toward the body being that of a foreign prince, a man who died while in Egypt and could not be returned to his home for burial. This theory was retracted due to the lack of identity and the fact that despite possible royal links, he would, as a foreigner, not have been placed alongside Egyptian pharaohs.

Below: Those who study the Screaming Mummy know that he died in agony, and—thanks to a CT scan like this one being done on another mummy—was Egyptian, possibly even royalty.

Over 100 years later, a CT scan of the skeletal remains indicated that the body was Egyptian and that it was indeed royalty, as implied by the shape of the skull. The shape, proportions, and the long distance of the cranium from the forehead to the back of the skull were in keeping with features of Egyptian royalty.

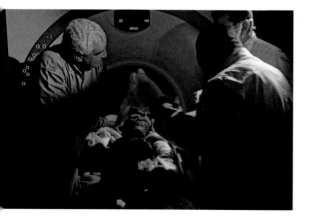

Into the twenty-first century, those who study the Screaming Mummy are left with a body buried with little care that belonged to someone who died in great pain. Not only that, but the body seems to belong to Egyptian royalty. For over 120 years, the body has intrigued and baffled in equal measure.

— ALTERNATIVE —
THEORIES

Armed with the theory that the Screaming Mummy was indeed royalty, experts directed their gaze to Pentawer, an Ancient Egyptian prince thought to have lived between 1173 BCE and 1155 BCE. Pentawer was the son of Pharaoh Ramesses III, and it is said he was involved in a plot to kill the pharaoh in order to come to power. DNA tests, while inconclusive, suggested that the mystery mummy was indeed related to Ramesses, but the nature of the plot and the manner in which the Screaming Mummy was killed are still shrouded in speculation.

It is said that the plot involved Pentawer, his mother Tiye, army commanders, and even the numerous women in the prince's harem. Whether or not the assassination plot was successful remains a mystery, although new evidence suggests the pharaoh's neck was slit. Records though suggest he lived until his 60s and died of ill health.

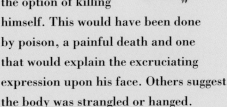

Right: Did Ramesses III have his throat slit by his own son, and could his son be the Screaming Mummy?

The theory goes on to argue that Pentawer was found guilty of the crime, but because of his noble background, was spared a gruesome execution (it is thought his co-conspirators were burned alive and their ashes strewn across the streets) and instead was afforded the option of killing himself. This would have been done by poison, a painful death and one that would explain the excruciating expression upon his face. Others suggest the body was strangled or hanged.

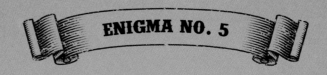

DID ADOLF HITLER DIE IN HIS BERLIN BUNKER?

Date: April 30, 1945
Location: Berlin, Germany

Did Adolf Hitler die in his bunker in the final days of World War II in Europe, or did he manage to escape and live out his days in South America?

On the evening of April 30, 1945, the German Chancellor Adolf Hitler and his wife Eva Braun are believed to have committed suicide in their bunker, 30 feet (9 meters) below Berlin. Eight days earlier, as the Soviet army advanced on Berlin and it was clear Germany had lost the war, Hitler began to hatch his plan to kill himself, and announced to his aides that he would remain in his bunker until the very end. He sought advice from SS physician Dr. Werner Haase about how he should end his life and was recommended the "pistol and poison method"—consuming a dose of cyanide and shooting himself in the head.

By April 28, the Soviets were in Berlin, and so, in one of his final acts, Hitler married Eva Braun inside the map room of the bunker, just after midnight of the following day. He had prepared for the

wedding by detailing his last will and testament to his personal secretary, Traudl Junge, which included the order that his body was to be cremated after his death. At 1 a.m. on April 29, Hitler and Eva Braun were married, with his close friend and Minister for Propaganda, Joseph Goebbels, as best man. A small party followed, where the guests drank champagne, but Hitler was busy dictating his will before he retired to bed at around 4 a.m.

Later that day, Hitler had learned that his former ally, the Italian dictator Benito Mussolini, had been killed alongside his mistress Clara Petacci, and their bodies strung up in the streets of Milan. Hitler was terrified he would suffer the same fate with his new wife when Berlin fell in the coming days. "He was depressed and suspicious of everybody," General Bernd Freytag von Loringhoven, who was with Hitler in the bunker, recalled. "He even now suspected that the poison would only make him unconscious and he'd be turned over alive to the Allies, so he decided to test the poison." Hitler gave a capsule of cyanide to his pet dog Blondi, who quickly died.

Above: Hitler, pictured here with Braun and their dogs ca. 1940, tested his cyanide on one of his dogs in the bunker.

SUSPECTED SUICIDE

On the morning of April 30, Hitler held meetings with his generals, who confirmed that defeat was unavoidable and that the Soviets were just 200 yards (180 meters) from the bunker. After Hitler and Braun ate a lunch of spaghetti with cabbage and raisin salad, Braun put on her husband's favorite dress and at 2:30 p.m. the pair retired to his personal study to kill themselves. At 3:30 p.m., there were reports that a gunshot had been heard from the study, and several officers, including Goebbels, opened the door to Hitler's study, to find the couple's corpses.

"We found Eva Braun sitting on the sofa, her head resting on Hitler's left shoulder," leader of the Hitler Youth, Artur Axmann, recalled. "She was dead, but had no marks of violence on her body. She died of the poison. Hitler's lower jaw was slightly discarded. It was obvious he had shot himself in the mouth. On either side of his temples I saw drops of blood. The blanks of his pistol had ruptured the veins on either side of his head. The sofa was stained with blood and the pistol lay at his feet. I remained with the corpses for about 10 minutes, then I returned to the conference room, and at this point saw Hitler's and Eva Braun's bodies being carried out of the bunker."

As instructed, Hitler's and Eva Braun's bodies were taken to the surface, to the garden behind the Reich Chancellery, covered in petrol, and burned. The bodies did not burn entirely and the remains were covered up and left in a shallow bomb crater. Two days later the Soviet army discovered these remains and soon after, in consultation with dental records, determined that this was Hitler and Braun. The remains would be buried and exhumed several times in three different locations before being left in an unmarked grave in a secret location. It wasn't until 1956 that Germany officially declared that Hitler was dead.

This is the course of events accepted by most historians, but almost immediately it was subjected to doubts and a campaign of disinformation that suggested Hitler had in fact survived, and managed to escape from Berlin. Even when President Harry Truman asked the Soviet leader Joseph Stalin whether Hitler was dead, at the Potsdam Conference in August 1945, he was told "No." The former supreme commander of the allies, Dwight D. Eisenhower, who would become US President in 1953, said, "We have been unable to unearth one bit of tangible evidence of Hitler's death. Many people believe he escaped from Berlin."

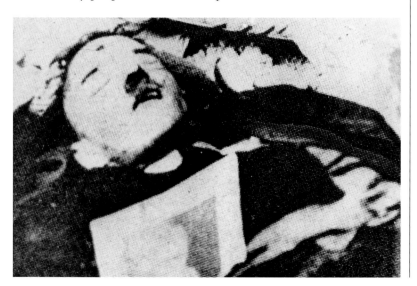

Left: Initially believed to be evidence of Hitler's death, this photo is now said to be a fake propaganda device fabricated by the Soviets' Red Army.

Above: Were the pair accompanied by Braun's brother-in-law, Hermann Fegelein, to a Junkers-52 transport aircraft, piloted by Captain Peter Baumgart?

ESCAPE TO SOUTH AMERICA?

In the years since, two English writers, Gerrard Williams and Simon Dunstan, have promoted the theory Hitler fled to South America. It is their belief that on the evening of April 27, 1945, Hitler and Braun escaped from the bunker by a secret tunnel. They were flown to Denmark, then to Spain, where General Franco provided a plane to fly to the Canary Islands, where they boarded a submarine which crossed the Atlantic to Argentina, and the small port of Necochea, 300 miles (480 kilometers) to the south of the capital, Buenos Aires. The authors purport that Hitler lived out the final years of his life in Argentina, and had two daughters with Eva Braun, before he died on February 13, 1962.

So, who were the bodies found by the Soviet Army? They were two body doubles dressed in Hitler's and Braun's clothes, to lead the Soviets and the Allies to believe they had been killed. Those who refused to believe Hitler perished in the bunker were buoyed in 2009, when it was discovered that a skull featuring a bullet hole in the temple, which had been found in May 1946 in the same crater as Hitler's other remains and had always been believed to be that of the dictator, in fact belonged to a woman less than 40 years old. The skull had been stored in the Russian state archives until 1993, but in 2009, Nick Bellantoni, an archaeologist and bone specialist, took DNA from the skull in Moscow and tested it at the University of Connecticut. It was not Hitler's and was not believed to be Eva Braun's either, as it was always reported she had died through cyanide and not a gunshot.

It has always been the discovery of Hitler's jaw that is proffered as conclusive proof that he had died, but few have examined it, and it is believed to be in the Lubyanka, the Russian secret police headquarters in Moscow.

— ALTERNATIVE —
THEORIES

In 2014 Simoni Renée Guerreiro Dias published a book entitled *Hitler in Brazil—His Life and Death*, in which she argues that the Nazi leader escaped to South America in 1945 and lived most of the rest of his life in Brazil, until he died in 1984 at the age of 95. She claims he went first to Argentina and then to Paraguay, before settling in the small Brazilian town of Nossa Senhora do Livramento where he went by the name of Adolf Leipzig and was known locally as the "Old German." It is suggested this man had a relationship with a local black woman called Cutinga, which would imply he did not share the racist Aryan views of the real Hitler, and so could not be him. A grainy picture of the couple exists, and, like the rest of this theory, remains inconclusive.

THE HUNT FOR HITLER

North Atlantic Ocean

BRAZIL

Nossa Senhora do Livramento

PARAGUAY

South Pacific Ocean

ARGENTINA

South Atlantic Ocean

Above: Did Hitler travel in South America, before settling in Brazil, having a relationship with a black woman, and dying at the age of 95?

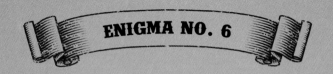

WHAT HAPPENED TO THE STUDENTS ON THE DYATLOV PASS?

Date: February 1959
Location: The Ural Mountains, Russia

A group of Russian students on a hiking trip are all found dead on the side of a snowy mountain, but why they fled their tent and how they perished remains a mystery.

On January 25, 1959, a group of 10 Russian students—all experienced hikers—set off on a journey to reach Mount Otorten in the northern Urals. When trip organizer Igor Dyatlov failed to send a telegram by February 12, to inform of the group's safe return to Vizhai, a search was launched. On February 26, the group's tent was discovered—empty. The entrance was closed, but the tent had been slashed open from the inside with a knife. Footprints led from the tent down the slope, and it was clear they had been left by the group either barefoot or only wearing socks. No one had been wearing boots. The footprints faded, then, on the edge of the woods on the opposite side of the pass, the first two bodies were found, underneath a large cedar tree.

Krivonischenko and Doroshenko were wearing only underwear and were next to what appeared to be a burned-out fire, while in the tree above several branches had been removed. Not far from them, three more bodies were found—Dyatlov, Slobodin, and Kolmogorova—who looked to have been attempting to return to the tent. After his death, the pass was named after Dyatlov. The cause of death for these five students was hypothermia, as they had been inadequately dressed and exposed to sub-zero temperatures estimated to have been between -13 and -22°F (-25 and -30°C).

It was more than two months later before the remaining four bodies were discovered, under 13 feet (4 meters) of snow in a ravine in the forest. Three of the four had fatal injuries: Thibeaux-Brignolles had died of a skull injury, Dubinina and Zolotaryov had major chest fractures, and Dubinina was also missing her eyeballs and tongue. Kolevatov was found alongside them. According to Dr. Boris Vozrozhdenny, who took part in the official inquest, these four students had died from "an unknown compelling force," which he likened to being in a car crash.

Above: The tomb of the fated group, in the Mikhailov Cemetery in Yekaterinburg, is a stark reminder of young lives cut tragically short.

WHY DID THEY LEAVE THEIR TENT?
An investigation found no signs of a struggle, and no sign that other people or an animal had been involved in the incident. The case was closed in May 1959, without drawing any definitive conclusions as to what had made these students flee from their tent, and how the four fatally injured in the ravine had died. This effectively exonerated the native Mansi people, a peaceful tribe, who some thought might have attacked the group for being on their land. Fanciful speculation that a yeti or large animal had killed them could also be easily dismissed.

An avalanche was also put forward as a reason for the group's rapid exit of their tent: they were in a panic, cut their way out as snow had covered the entrance, and didn't have time to put on their clothes and boots. Five of the group had died from exposure; the other four had been killed by being caught in the full force of the avalanche. Dubinina's missing tongue and eyeballs could be explained as having been taken by a scavenging animal. Yet there were no obvious signs of an avalanche, the area was not covered by an unusually heavy amount of snow, and it had no history of avalanches.

Another theory was that an infrasound noise created by wind traveling around the mountain had induced a collective panic attack in the group, forcing them to leave their tent. Five of them had died from exposure, and the other four had slipped into the ravine and landed on the rocks below. A less dramatic and more plausible theory is that the group had been forced to leave their tent when sparks from their stove had started a fire, and they were forced to cut their way out as the fire spread. Some members of the group were found with singed hands. Their footprints in the snow, however, showed that on leaving the tent they were calm and not in a rush, as they went to seek shelter in the forest below.

Below: A view of the tent as the rescuers found it, cut open from inside. The photograph was taken by Soviet authorities.

— ALTERNATIVE —
THEORIES

The theory that has caused the most interest, and has never been ruled out, is that the group were the victims of a secret military test. There were records of parachute mines being tested in this area, which would detonate before they hit the ground. Could this have forced the group to leave their tent in such haste? Another group of hikers 30 miles (48 kilometers) away reported that they had seen glowing orange globes in the sky where Dyatlov and his group had made their campsite. The chief investigator Lev Ivanov commented in 1990 that, "I suspected at the time and I am almost sure that these bright flying spheres had a direct connection to

Above: Did the group perish in an accident caused by the military, who were testing in this area of the Urals?

their deaths." Some of the group were also found to have a surprisingly high level of radiation on their clothes, while others reported that five of the group had unusually tanned faces. In 2008, six former rescuers and 31 independent experts, who gathered at Yekaterinburg at a conference convened by the Ural State Technical University and the Dyatlov Foundation, concluded that military tests in the area had caused the deaths of the group.

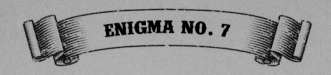
WAS THE BIMINI ROAD MADE BY NATURE OR MAN?

Date: Discovered in 1968
Location: North Bimini Island, the Bahamas

Underneath the water is an almost perfect road made of rocks, but is it a quirk of nature or could it have been made by man, and even be a part of the lost city of Atlantis?

On September 2, 1968, a trio of subsea archaeologists—Jacques Mayol, Robert Angove, and Joseph Manson Valentine—were 18 feet (5.5 meters) beneath the water, off the northwest coast of North Bimini Island, when they discovered what appeared to be a road on the bed of the ocean. They proclaimed they had found a "pavement," now commonly known as the Bimini Road. This road ran for just under half a mile (a kilometer) on a northeast-southwest line and consisted of limestone blocks aligned in precise geometric patterns. The blocks appeared to have been cut into a rectangular shape and some of the beachrock appeared to have been stacked to level out the road. The road ends with a hooked shape, which gives the appearance of the letter "J" from above. It was later discovered that there were two smaller roads in a similar design parallel to the Bimini Road.

A series of tests have determined that the rocks are around 3,500 years old, and that the current surface was exposed by natural erosion around 1,900–2,000 years ago. The discovery of this road triggered a debate as to whether this was a natural collection of rocks or whether somehow it was a manmade structure, which had then been submerged by water.

"There is sand on one side and sand on the other on what is a clear defined pathway," the marine biologist Dr. Michael Haley, who has visited the underwater road, has said. "There are rectilinear 90-degree angles which you don't find in nature and is very unusual. The support rocks also don't make sense. Most people would conclude that humans have placed it there and used the support rocks to level it out. No one who sees the road can think it is not a manmade artifact."

However, a consensus among archaeologists and geologists has emerged that the Bimini Road was created through the beachrock naturally forming in this pattern on the bed of the ocean. It is a long and detailed process, but it is normal for beachrock to crack into a tile-like rock that gives the impression of being manmade.

THE ROAD TO ATLANTIS

However, for many, the rocks fit together too perfectly and appear to have been cut by humans—and they are desperate to prove it. In 1980 some samples taken from the Bimini Road were found to have micrite, aragonite,

Below: Over time, the edges of the beachrock of the Bimini Road, which is native to the Bahamas, have rounded off.

Above: The sunken city of Atlantis is one of the world's most enduring legends, first mentioned in Plato's *Timaeus* and *Critias*, in which the Athenians, after defeating the Atlanteans, incur the wrath of the gods, and Atlantis sinks into the sea, never to be found.

and calcite in them, which are not normally found in beachrock and suggest it could have been manmade. In 2006 Dr. Greg Little took a team of researchers to the Bimini Road to find evidence to support his theory that it was manmade. Some geologists have contended that only sand and water should be beneath the Bimini rocks, but Little and his team found a second layer of what appeared to be cut rocks in similar dimensions, supporting his theory it was manmade.

There is a willingness to believe these theories, as it would mean the Bimini Road could have formed a part of the lost city of Atlantis. Fueling this is a prediction from the American psychic Edgar Cayce, who was a great believer that the city would be discovered. In 1938 Cayce said: "A portion of the temples may yet be discovered under the slime of ages and seawater near Bimini," he said. "Expect it in '68 or '69." The fact that the Bimini Road was discovered in 1968 has cemented the views of Atlantis believers, who claim this is simply the first of these structures to be discovered. However, according to Plato, Atlantis was around 9,000 years old, and the rocks in the road were found to be about 3,500 years old, so even allowing for some margin of error, they would be far too recent.

—ALTERNATIVE—
THEORIES

The historian Gavin Menzies has developed his own theory, suggesting that the road was manmade in the fifteenth century by the Chinese, which he details in his book *1421: The Year China Discovered America*. According to Menzies, between 1421 and 1423 the Chinese admiral Zheng He was caught in a severe storm near Bimini. To repair the damaged ships in his fleet, the rest of the fleet created a dry dock using their large, rectangular ballast stones to haul damaged junks ashore for refitting and repairs. It is believed that sea levels were 6 feet (2 meters) lower in the 1400s, and so Menzies suggested that the rocks that form the Bimini Road were once on North Bimini Island.

Right: Zheng He may have been sailing around the world with an imperial fleet and exploring the Caribbean between 1421 and 1423—did he build the road?

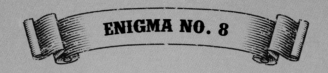

WHO ELSE SHOT ROBERT F. KENNEDY?

Date: June 5, 1968
Location: Los Angeles

While running to be president, the New York senator was shot in Los Angeles, but only one man has ever been convicted of his killing. Was there another gunman?

On the evening of June 4, 1968, Senator Robert F. Kennedy was declared the winner of the California and South Dakota primaries in his bid to win the Democratic nomination for President of the United States. Kennedy now had the second most delegates behind Vice President Hubert Humphrey, but, crucially, also had the momentum, which many believed would now sweep him to the nomination and on to the White House in November.

It was a time of great social unrest in the US, just two months after the assassination of civil rights leader Martin Luther King, with riots in several cities and the increasingly unpopular Vietnam War—which had caused President Lyndon B. Johnson not to seek reelection.

Above: Kennedy was seen by many, especially the young and disadvantaged, as a genuine beacon of hope.

In the Embassy Ballroom at the Ambassador Hotel in Los Angeles, flanked by his pregnant wife, Ethel, Kennedy delivered a victory speech to his campaign supporters before finishing by saying, "My thanks to all of you, and now it's on to Chicago, and let's win there." Just after midnight, Kennedy left the stage and made his way through an adjoining kitchen, where supporters and hotel workers clamored to shake his hand. Sirhan Sirhan had been hiding in between an ice machine and a stack of trays before he stepped out and fired a .22 caliber Iver Johnson Cadet revolver three times at Kennedy from close range.

One bullet entered Kennedy's head behind his right ear, one went through the back of his armpit and chest, and the third and final bullet stayed in the back of his neck. The wounded senator fell to the floor and Sirhan fired his final five bullets at five others in the kitchen, none of whom were fatally wounded, before one of Kennedy's bodyguards, William Barry, disarmed the gunman. Barry placed his jacket under Kennedy's head as he lay on the floor, and knew it was serious when he saw the hole in his head. Busboy Juan Romero, who had only just shaken Kennedy's hand, now cradled his head as the senator asked, "Is everybody okay?" Romero said they were, before Kennedy added, "Everything's going to be okay." Within minutes medics arrived at Kennedy's

Below: Kennedy lies on the floor of the Ambassador Hotel after being shot; busboy Juan Romero is among those aiding him.

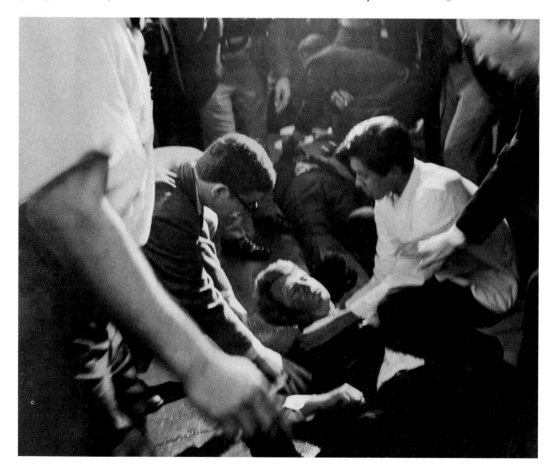

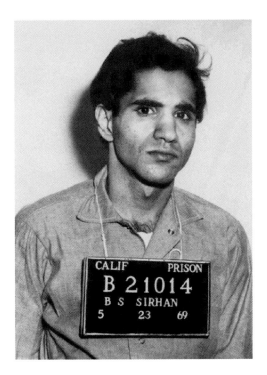

Above: Sirhan Sirhan has been denied parole several times, and has now spent 50 years in prison.

side, and they lifted him onto a stretcher, provoking him to wince and say quietly, "Don't lift me." These would prove to be his last words, as just over 24 hours later, at 1:44 a.m. on June 6, he succumbed to his gunshot wounds and was declared dead at the Hospital of the Good Samaritan in Los Angeles.

PRIME SUSPECT

Sirhan Sirhan was a 22-year-old Palestinian with Jordanian citizenship, who had been born in Jerusalem and had seemingly wanted to kill Kennedy for his public support of the state of Israel. During a search of his home, the police found a diary in which he had written an entry on May 19: "My determination to eliminate R. F. K. is becoming more and more of an unshakable obsession. R. F. K. must die. R. F. K. must be killed. Robert F. Kennedy must be assassinated ... Robert F. Kennedy must be assassinated before June 5 '68." On the night of the assassination, Sirhan was found to have a newspaper cutting in his pocket that discussed Kennedy's support of Israel.

Sirhan had shot Kennedy in front of a room full of about 30 witnesses, and was disarmed and arrested at the scene. A seemingly open and shut case. On April 17, 1969, Sirhan was convicted of murder and sentenced to death six days later, but in 1972 it was commuted to life in prison when the California Supreme Court outlawed the death penalty. At first glance, it would appear that Kennedy's assassination, in contrast to his brother's assassination five years earlier, was a straightforward affair. While Sirhan clearly played a role in Kennedy's death, there have always been credible theories that he did not act alone.

UNLIKELY LONE ASSASSIN

The location of Kennedy's gunshot wounds pointed to the shooter being behind him, yet it was reported that Sirhan was in front of him. The Los Angeles coroner Thomas Noguchi declared that the fatal shot was behind Kennedy's right ear, fired from a distance of around 1 inch (2.5 cm), but witnesses have placed Sirhan around 18 inches (45 cm) away when he fired his shots. The lead crime scene investigator DeWayne Wolfer testified at Sirhan's trial that a bullet from Kennedy's body was from Sirhan's gun, but this was contradicted by other experts who said the bullet in Kennedy and two other victims were from different guns and bullets. An internal police document even concluded that, "Kennedy and Weisel [the ABC producer who was also hit] bullets not fired from same gun," and, "Kennedy bullet not fired from Sirhan's revolver." This prompted the city of Los Angeles to appoint Special Counsel Thomas F. Kranz to investigate the assassination, but he found no evidence to suggest that there was a second gunman, and concluded Sirhan acted alone.

In 2004 the Polish journalist Stanisław Pruszyński discovered he had the only audio recording of the assassination and passed his cassette to the audio engineer Philip van Praag, who found that 13, not 8, shots had been fired. "The conclusion is inescapable," Van Praag wrote in 2011, "that there was a second gun fired by a second shooter during the shooting that resulted in the death of Senator Robert F. Kennedy, and that the five shots from the second gun were fired in a direction opposite the direction in which Sirhan fired." Other witnesses in the kitchen reported hearing more than eight shots, somewhere between 10 and 14. Even Kennedy's son, Robert F. Kennedy Junior, believes that two guns were fired that night, "There were too many bullets, you can't fire 13 shots out of an 8-shot gun."

— ALTERNATIVE —
THEORIES

There is enough doubt to suggest Sirhan Sirhan did not act alone, but it remains unresolved who else could have killed Kennedy. In 2006, while making a documentary for the BBC, Shane O'Sullivan found new evidence that placed three senior CIA officers at the hotel that night. One of these men was David Morales, who O'Sullivan claims once boasted in 1973, "I was in Dallas when we got the son of a bitch [JFK], and I was in Los Angeles when we got the little bastard." Another of the men O'Sullivan identified was found to have died in 1962, six years before Kennedy was assassinated.

The third man, Thane Eugene Cesar, was a security guard standing behind Kennedy when he was killed, and as the Senator was shot from behind, suspicion fell on him that he could be the second gunman. Cesar gave conflicting accounts of his movements, and several witnesses saw him pull his gun; one believed he fired it. Cesar has always denied he had anything to do with the assassination.

Right: The presence of a woman in a polka dot dress at the hotel on the night has long been the source of much intrigue.

A worker on the Kennedy campaign, Sandro Serrano, around 45 minutes before the senator was killed, reported seeing a woman in a polka dot dress with someone she later identified as Sirhan Sirhan. At 12:15 a.m., immediately after the shots were fired, Serrano saw the woman in the polka dot dress running from the scene shouting, "We shot him, we shot him!" Other witnesses also reported seeing the woman, but more than half a century later she has never been identified.

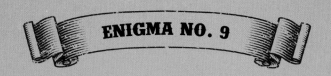
WHAT CAUSED THE CHILDREN OF THE HOLLINWELL INCIDENT TO COLLAPSE?

Date: July 13, 1980
Location: Kirkby-in-Ashfield, Nottinghamshire, England

In a field near Nottingham nearly 300 children attending a competition collapsed due to a mysterious illness that is still baffling experts.

On a summer's day in 1980, the Forest League of Juvenile Jazz Bands staged a charity competition for children's brass bands at the Hollinwell showground near Kirkby-in-Ashfield. A total of around 500 children from 11 marching bands were entered in the Junior Brass and Marching Band competition, which began at 9 a.m. From around 10:30 a.m., and for the next two hours, nearly 300 children, as well as several accompanying adults, would mysteriously collapse in the field.

Left: The showground was littered with the bodies of children—a policeman said, "there were bodies everywhere."

Terry Bingham was an organizer for one of the bands and has recalled the scene that unfolded around him: "We were ready for the display when one or two children collapsed. Then a few more went, and a few more. We called off the event, but others fell as they came out of the arena. Then spectators started dropping."

Petula Merriman was 14 years old at the time and has recalled her traumatic experience that day: "We were on the field for a full inspection. I have never had to stand to attention for that long before. As we marched off I tried to grab hold of my drum, but just fell to the floor. My friends were collapsing all around me." Kerry Elliot, 10 years old, was also there: "I went all weak and got pains in my stomach and then fainted. Everyone was falling down and some were crying. My stomach was all tight and aching." The lead drummer in her band, Susan Rook, was 13 at the time, and said: "My legs and arms felt as if they had no bones in them and I had a bad headache."

A BATTLEFIELD

All the victims have described their symptoms as fainting, running eyes, a sore throat, dizziness, vomiting, and numbness, and some have spoken about having a metallic taste in their mouth.

A policeman at the scene has said, "The kids went down like ninepins … it was like a battlefield." A total of 259 people would be taken to four hospitals; most were released that night, but nine were kept in for observation.

What could have made so many people suddenly collapse? The official inquiry blamed the rather vague notion of mass hysteria, when people can collectively experience fainting, abdominal pain, nausea, headaches, and hyperventilation. Crucially, these outbreaks only last for around two hours. Dr. John Wood, the director of health for the Kirkby area, said, "Part of it may have been one or two people feeling ill and the rest getting hysteria."

WAS THERE A COVER-UP?

Into the vacuum stepped a host of theories. There were suggestions the children could have been affected by an unusually strong strain of food poisoning, yet there was no evidence that they had eaten the same food. Could the water drunk by them in the field have been contaminated? Again, there was no evidence.

There were suggestions that an aggressive mystery bug had swept through the field, as a few of the children had marks on their skin similar to chicken pox. The police were aware of a fire at a nearby plastics factory, but it was discovered that the wind had been moving in the opposite direction to the field.

"There has been a cover-up," said Terry Bingham, soon after the inquiry. "Some people are still feeling ill, so how can it have been mass hysteria?" On the day, it was reported that two horses had also become unwell and collapsed, and a week later, *The Sunday Times* reported that five horses at a nearby horse competition had become unwell and had to be destroyed. Could something still have been in the air?

Right: In 2000 the British government banned the use of tridemorph, and the World Health Organization classified it as a "moderately hazardous" pesticide.

Below: A doctor nominated the Coxsackie virus as the cause of the incident but offered little to support this.

ALTERNATIVE THEORIES

In 2003 the BBC's *Inside Out* investigations team found that the now-banned chemical tridemorph had been sprayed on crops in the nearby fields in the days before the incident. One of the side effects of tridemorph is that it can cause skin and eye irritations—could a heavy dose have poisoned the children?

Steve Mitchell was an ambulance worker who rushed to the field to attend to the many victims and has suggested a chemical played a role in the incident: "There were a lot of young people very distressed—their eyes were very sore and [they] had severe breathing difficulties; there was a smell in the air. With the bands marching up and down, they were dispersing the chemical into the air, and I am sure it was inhaled by the young children."

The 1980 inquiry by Ashfield District Council found that the pesticide Calixin, which contains tridemorph, had been sprayed on neighboring fields in the week leading up to the incident, but it was ruled that this had no impact.

Since then, the politician Dennis Skinner has said that citing mass hysteria as the cause of the incident was "an insult to the intelligence and another cover-up by the Establishment." Despite pressure from Parliament and parents, Ashfield District Council has refused to reopen the case, and the mystery of why so many children collapsed in that field in 1980 remains unsolved.

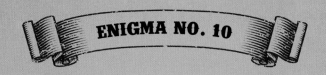

WHAT LIT UP RENDLESHAM FOREST?

Date: December 26–28, 1980
Location: Suffolk, England

A series of bright lights in the sky above a forest and an American Air Force base in southeast England has never been properly explained.

Rendlesham Forest is an unremarkable 3,700 acres (1,500 hectares) of mixed woodland in Suffolk, UK, but in 1980 it would become forever famous as the site of Britain's best-known potential UFO sighting. At around 3 a.m. on December 26, a security patrol consisting of two men, John Burroughs and James Penniston, from RAF Woodbridge, a military base being used by the United States Air Forces (USAF), reported seeing a set of lights descend beneath the trees in the forest.

According to a memo from the deputy base commander Lieutenant Colonel Charles Halt, the servicemen, on entering the forest, saw a glowing metal object, which soon began to move through the trees. One of the servicemen, James Penniston, even claimed to have touched what he described as "a craft of unknown origin."

When it became light, the servicemen returned to the scene and noticed three significant marks in the dirt on the ground in a triangular pattern. Could some form of alien spaceship have landed there during the night?

In the early hours of December 28, Halt took a group of servicemen back to this area of the forest to seek radiation readings, but nothing proved conclusive. While they were in the forest, Halt reported seeing flashing lights in between the trees and three bright lights in the sky, which remained there for around three hours.

COORDINATED COVER-UP?

A month later, Lieutenant Colonel Halt would compose a memo entitled "Unexplained Lights," but the British Ministry of Defence never felt there was anything of genuine interest nor any threat to national security in this memo that would justify launching a full-scale investigation. The Suffolk police were also called to the forest on both occasions in December, both at night and in daylight, and found nothing of interest. A frustrated Halt has since claimed he witnessed an event "extra-terrestrial in origin," but that the UK and US governments did not take him seriously and engaged in a massive cover-up.

Below: The hangars at the air base at RAF Woodbridge in Rendlesham Forest now stand abandoned.

In 2015 Halt claimed he now had statements from radar operators at RAF Bentwaters, which was also used by the USAF, and Wattisham Airfield that they had picked up an unidentified object. "I have confirmation [Bentwaters radar operators] … saw the object go across their 60-mile scope in two or three seconds, thousands of miles an hour, [it] came back across their scope again, stopped near the water tower, they watched it and observed it go into the forest where we were," Halt said. "At Wattisham, they picked up what they called a 'bogie' and lost it near Rendlesham Forest. Whatever was there was clearly under intelligent control."

At the time, Holt's superior at the base, Colonel Ted Conrad, went to the forest the day after the lights had been seen, and to the area where the markings had been found, but says he found them "unremarkable." On the second night, when lights were claimed to have been seen, Conrad was in radio contact with his deputy Halt, who was in the forest and reported he could see lights in the sky and through the trees. On the base not far away, Conrad himself looked up at the sky, but recalls seeing nothing out of the ordinary. "We saw nothing that resembled Lieutenant Colonel Halt's descriptions either in the sky or on the ground," Colonel Conrad said in 2011, when he spoke publicly for the first time about the incident. "We had people in position to validate Halt's narrative, but none of them could. He should be ashamed and embarrassed by his allegation that his country and England both conspired to deceive their citizens … He knows better. I think the odds are way high against there being an ET spacecraft involved, and almost equally high against it being an intrusion of hostile earthly craft."

— ALTERNATIVE —
THEORIES

In 2003 former USAF security policeman Kevin Conde claimed he had played a prank on his colleagues at RAF Woodbridge. He and another airman had shone patrol-car lights through the trees and made noises on a loudspeaker. "It was fertile ground for a practical joke, which are a tradition in the security police," Conde said. He explained he was moved to another base soon after, so took a long time to realize his prank had been so successful.

Above: A regularly flashing, bright, and beaming light sounds just like that of a local lighthouse…

Another possible explanation is that the lights came from nearby Orford Ness Lighthouse. On December 28, Halt said that the light he saw was in the same direction as two nights earlier, and, crucially, flashed every five seconds, the pattern from Orford Ness. As Inspector Mike Topliss, who helped investigate the incident, said, "The immediate area was swept by powerful light beams from a landing beacon at RAF Bentwaters and the Orford Ness Lighthouse. I know from personal experience that at night, in certain weather and cloud conditions, these beams were very pronounced, and certainly caused strange visual effects."

Rather than a UFO, the lights could also be explained by a fireball in the sky, a series of bright stars, or a falling satellite. And the marks on the ground were identified by police as rabbit diggings, and not proof that a UFO had landed in the forest.

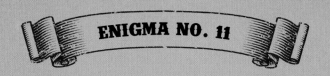

HOW DID THE SEVERED FEET OF THE SALISH SEA END UP THERE?

Date: 2007–Present day
Location: British Columbia, Canada, and Washington State

Over more than a decade, as many as 19 human feet have washed up on the shores of the Pacific northwest of Canada and the United States, and no one knows where they came from.

The first foot was discovered at the end of August 2007, when a family from Washington were enjoying a day trip to a beach on Jedediah Island, off the coast of British Columbia. Their 12-year-old daughter found a blue-and-white size 12 Campus running shoe. She picked it up and immediately realized it was heavier than it should have been; inside was a wet sock that contained the remains of a human foot.

Six days later, Michele Geris and George Baugh were hiking on Gabriola Island, 18 miles (30 kilometers) south of Jedediah Island, when Michele spotted a Reebok shoe. Inside were the remains of a foot encased in a sock.

"Two being found in such a short period of time is quite suspicious," Garry Cox of the Oceanside Royal Canadian Mounted Police told *The Vancouver Sun*. "Finding one foot is like a million to one odds, but to find two is crazy. I've heard of dancers with two left feet, but come on."

The feet would appear in steady succession—after the initial two, a glut of five of them in 2008, one in 2009, two in 2010, three in 2011, one in 2012, one in 2014, two in 2016, one in 2017, and one in 2018. Fourteen of the feet have been found in Canada, with the other five to the south, in the United States. The most recent find occurred in May 2018, when a man walking along a beach on Gabriola Island on a Sunday lunchtime found a hiking boot, with a human foot inside, lodged among some logs.

It baffled investigators and local authorities that only feet were being washed up on beaches, and not other body parts. And why were they mainly right feet, and most wearing running shoes?

Below: There has been such a steady stream of feet that it is possible to map them.

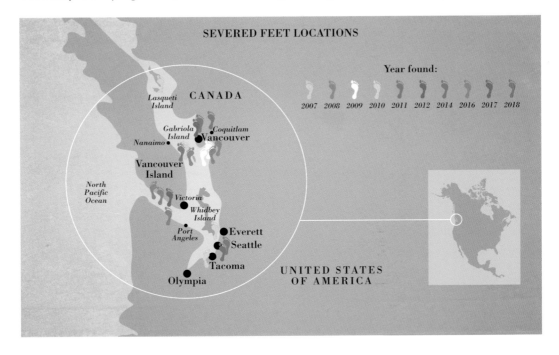

SEVERED FEET LOCATIONS

Year found:

2007 2008 2009 2010 2011 2012 2014 2016 2017 2018

CANADA

Lasqueti Island

Gabriola Island *Coquitlam* Vancouver

Nanaimo •

Vancouver Island

North Pacific Ocean

Victoria

Whidbey Island

Port Angeles • Everett

• Seattle

• Tacoma

• Olympia

UNITED STATES OF AMERICA

PLANE CRASH OR NATURAL DISASTER?

In February 2005, five men had drowned after their MJM Air de Havilland Beaver float plane had crashed minutes after take-off from Tyee Spit and sunk off Quadra Island in Canada. The bodies of four of the men were never found, and so it was speculated that their feet had become loose over time in the water and washed up on the beaches over the years; but when more and more feet began appearing, this theory had to be dismissed.

Writer Shane Lambert promoted the theory that several of the feet belonged to victims of the Asian Tsunami of 2004, who had been pulled out to sea. Lambert contends that the bodies floated in the ocean for several years before being dragged through the Pacific, with their feet eventually washing up on the shores of Canada or the US. He believed that sharks and other marine life had eaten the

Above: Many people become lost at sea, for many reasons, but why have so many feet been washed up in the Salish Sea specifically?

Above: The 2004 tsunami killed an estimated 250,000 people when an earthquake on the bed of the Indian Ocean caused huge waves to crash into the shores of several countries, including Indonesia, Sri Lanka, Thailand, and India.

rest of the bodies, but the feet remained protected inside the shoes, which animals would not consume. Four of the shoes discovered in 2007 and 2008 had been manufactured before December 2004, when the tsunami occurred.

OR MURDER?

Another theory is that the severed feet were not the result of an accident, but more sinister foul play, having been cut from their victims by a serial killer, drug dealer, or a mafia hitman, and tossed into the water. However, none of the feet have shown any signs of being forcibly removed, and as Vancouver city coroner Stephen Fonseca, who studied many of them, said in 2011: "There's no evidence of mechanical disarticulation."

The feet had not been cut off with a saw or large knife, but rather they had naturally come apart from their bodies after being submerged in the water for a long time. Studies have shown that when a body is floating in the water, it is subjected to the push and pull of its environment and disintegrates, the soft tissue and bones of the hands and feet being the first to separate. While other body parts will be eaten by marine life and sink to the bottom of the ocean bed, feet that are in shoes will be protected—and the shoes, if they are running shoes, will act as floating devices.

However, some, including Mark Mendelson, a forensics consultant and former Toronto police detective, are convinced that the owners of these feet met a grisly end: "Even a bad episode of *The Sopranos* will cough up a couple of other body parts than feet," Mendelson said. "There are so many coincidences taking place, I don't think you can write it off. Everybody who jumps off a bridge [to commit suicide] is wearing runners? It's bizarre. The common denominators are such that you've got to wonder. Until you can show me something pathologically concrete that this is a natural separation of that foot from a body, then I'm saying you've got to think dirty."

Below: Modern running shoes are kept buoyant by the gas-filled chambers in the soles.

— ALTERNATIVE —
THEORIES

Some of the feet have been identified as belonging to people it is believed committed suicide by jumping off local bridges. One foot, found on the banks of the Fraser River in 2007, belonged to a man from Surrey, British Columbia, who was suffering from mental illness and had not been seen by his family since disappearing from his home earlier that year. Another severed foot was found to have come from a man from White Rock, British Columbia, who had suffered from schizophrenia and had experienced a breakdown after his medication failed to work. He was last seen by a bridge by the Fraser River, where his foot was found.

"All of the [feet] who've been identified so far, there's no mystery," Gail Anderson, a criminologist at British Columbia's Simon Fraser University, said in 2011. "These people were very depressed, unhappy about life, and were last seen heading toward the water. People jump off bridges. They deliberately wish to disappear."

Above: "People jump off bridges"—and here are just three of the many that span the Fraser River: the Sky Bridge, the Pattullo Bridge, and the Railway Bridge.

This is still guesswork: there is no evidence the owners of these identified feet committed suicide. And why these feet keep appearing in this area of the Pacific northwest has never been adequately answered, only serving to fuel the mystery.

MYSTERIOUS DISAPPEARANCES

This chapter investigates the disappearances of a racehorse, a popstar, a young pilot, a group of cosmonauts, and the crew of two ships. The whereabouts of these subjects continues to fascinate and confound any rational explanation.

Disappearances at sea play to our deepest fears about the vastness of the ocean. In 1921 a commercial schooner was found run aground off the coast of North Carolina. Rescuers found no sign of the crew of 12 men. What happened to them? Two decades later, and the crew of the SS *Ourang Medan were* found, but with their faces contorted with terror—theirs is a different tale, but one of equal mystery.

Left: Did Russia's lost cosmonauts fall prey to the propaganda machine of the Cold War?

There are others who simply disappeared without a trace. Shergar was one of the most famous racehorses in the world, until he was kidnapped in February 1981, and was never seen again. In 1978 a young pilot went missing on a flight over Bass Strait, after telling air traffic control he was being chased by a strange flying object. Manic Street Preachers guitarist Richey Edwards had achieved huge success when he suddenly disappeared from a London hotel at the start of 1995; he has never been seen again. In the race to be the first nation to put men in space in the 1950s, it is believed the Soviet Union lost several of their cosmonauts in unsuccessful attempts, their disappearances never properly explained.

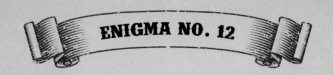
WHAT WAS THE FATE OF THE CREW OF THE CARROLL A. DEERING?

Date: January 1921
Location: Diamond Shoals, North Carolina

This schooner was returning from Brazil when it ran aground off the coast of North Carolina, but when rescuers boarded they found no sign of the crew.

On August 22, 1920, the *Carroll A. Deering*, a commercial schooner with five masts and which had only been built the previous year, set sail from Newport News, Virginia, to the Brazilian city of Rio de Janeiro, captained by William H. Merritt. It had a crew of 10 sailors, mostly from Denmark, and was carrying a cargo of coal, but a few days into the voyage, Captain Merritt complained of feeling unwell, and the boat docked at Lewes, Delaware, to let him disembark. A new captain, W. B. Wormell, and new first mate, Charles B. McLellan, were recruited so the ship could complete its journey.

Left: A grainy image of the *Carroll A. Deering* as seen from the Cape Lookout lightship on January 28, 1921, when Captain Jacobson saw the crew on the deck and sensed all was not well.

The *Deering* set off again on September 8, 1920, and reached Brazil, where it offloaded the coal, before starting its return journey to Virginia on December 2. In early January 1921, the *Deering* docked at Barbados to pick up supplies, and, as detailed in Bland Simpson's *Ghost Ship of Diamond Shoals: The Mystery of the Carroll A. Deering*, it was clear there was tension among the crew, especially between Captain Wormell and First Mate McLellan. On shore, Wormell complained to Captain Norton of the *Snow* about McLellan, saying, "He's been habitually drunk while ashore, and he's utterly unable to handle the crew properly. Here in Bridgetown [Barbados] he's been ashore drunk most of the time. He treats the men brutally, totally uncalled upon."

On that same day, Norton would also come across McLellan, who vented his annoyance at his crew and his captain, saying, "[I'm] having trouble with my crew ... they refuse to work. And times I have wanted to punish them, Captain Wormell steps in, interfering, interceding on their behalf, so I have got no authority, and can't do anything with them." McLellan would also complain about Wormell's increasingly poor eyesight. There would be three witnesses, including Norton, who would also hear McLellan threaten Wormell: "I'll get the captain before we get to Norfolk. I will."

ABANDONED SHIP

This clearly unhappy ship left Barbados for Hampton Roads, Virginia, on January 9, and nearly three weeks later was seen off the coast of North Carolina passing the Cape Lookout lightship. The *Deering* contacted Captain Jacobson on the lightship, and an unidentified crewman, whom he described as thin with reddish hair and with a foreign accent, told him that they had lost their anchors in a storm off Cape Fear. Jacobson was only able to note it and not report it as his radio was not working at that moment, but he was able to see that the crew were milling around on the foredeck of the ship—and something didn't feel right.

The very next day the *Deering* passed the SS *Lake Elon* southwest of the Diamond Shoals lightship at 5:45 p.m., and those who saw it commented on its strange course. Two days later, at 6:30 a.m.

on the morning of January 31, C. P. Brady of the Cape Hatteras coast guard station spotted the *Deering* aground on the Diamond Shoals, but rough seas prevented any boats reaching it until the morning of February 4.

Captain James Carlson of the *Rescue* was the first to board the *Deering*, and he immediately confirmed it had been abandoned. There was no crew on board. The ship's log, key navigational equipment, and personal belongings, including certain papers, were all missing. As previously reported, its anchors were missing, and the *Deering*'s two lifeboats were also gone. In the galley, food had been laid out as if the crew were about to sit down to eat. This macabre discovery prompted many questions—What had happened to the *Deering*? Where were the crew? Why had the ship been abandoned?—to which the authorities had no answers.

Below: The rough seas of Diamond Shoals initially prevented rescue boats from reaching the grounded *Deering*.

ANSWER IN A BOTTLE?

The first clue came later in April 1921, when Christopher Columbus Gray from Buxton, North Carolina, claimed to have found a message in a bottle at the beach. The message suggested the crew had been captured by pirates: "*Deering* captured by oil burning boat something like *Chaser*. Taking off everything handcuffing crew. Crew hiding all over ship no chance to make escape. Finder please notify headquarters *Deering*." At first it was suggested the note was written by the *Deering*'s engineer Herbert Bates, but Gray later admitted the message was an elaborate hoax and he had written it himself.

In May 1921, Captain Wormell's wife, Lula, Captain Merritt, who had started the journey, and Reverend Dr. Addison Lorimer made a trip to Washington, D.C., where they successfully petitioned Herbert Hoover, then the Secretary of Commerce, to launch an investigation. The investigation was headed up by Hoover's assistant, Lawrence Ritchey, and though he visited North Carolina himself, and enlisted the support of the FBI and several government departments, by the end of 1922 he was forced to close it without providing any official conclusion to the case.

Above: The sand-blasted wreckage of the ghost ship *Deering* lies just out of Bath, Maine, New England.

ALTERNATIVE
THEORIES

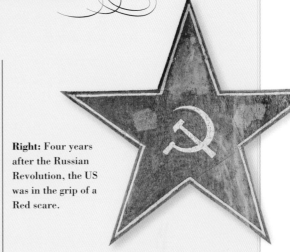

There were a couple of notable hurricanes happening in the Atlantic at the time the crew of the *Deering* disappeared. Could the crew have strayed into one and been thrown overboard, or tried to escape in the lifeboats and sunk? The *Deering*, however, was never in the direct path of the storm.

Right: Four years after the Russian Revolution, the US was in the grip of a Red scare.

Theories were advanced that communist sympathizers among the crew could have staged a mutiny, or communist agents might have boarded and taken control of the ship. The FBI had raided the United Russian Workers headquarters in New York and found evidence that Russia had ordered their agents to seize control of ships in American waters. If not Russian agents, there was a strong belief, advanced by Wormell's widow, that pirates operating in the area had seized the men and any valuables.

Or, could the crew have risen up and launched a mutiny? It was clear, through discussions both Wormell and McLellan had in Barbados, that all was not well on board. When the *Deering* contacted Captain Jacobson at Cape Lookout, he was certain he did not speak to Wormell, and that the man was not an officer. The US government's leading theory was that a mutiny had occurred.

The *Deering*, having sailed through the Bermuda Triangle, has always excitedly drawn the attention of those who promote the paranormal as an explanation, but the ship had successfully passed through the notorious Triangle, and was hundreds of miles away when it ran aground.

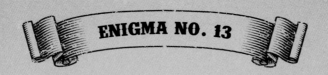

WHAT HAPPENED TO THE SS *OURANG MEDAN?*

Date: June 1947 or February 1948
Location: Straits of Malacca, Marshall Islands, or Solomon Islands

The crew of this ship were discovered dead on board, their faces frozen in terror. How did they come to die, and did the *Ourang Medan* ever even exist?

Nothing is certain about the fate of the Dutch ship SS *Ourang Medan*, not even when or where it was last seen. In either June 1947 or February 1948, a series of distress calls were made by the boat in the Straits of Malacca, between Indonesia and Sumatra. Other reports place the ship 400 miles (650 kilometers) southeast of the Marshall Islands in the Pacific Ocean; another report has it close to the Solomon Islands.

The US ships *Silver Star* and *City of Baltimore*, as well as English and Dutch listening posts, received this distress call in Morse code: "We float. All officers, including the captain, dead in the chartroom and on the bridge. Probably whole of crew dead." It was impossible to decipher what came next, until a second and final message arrived: "I die."

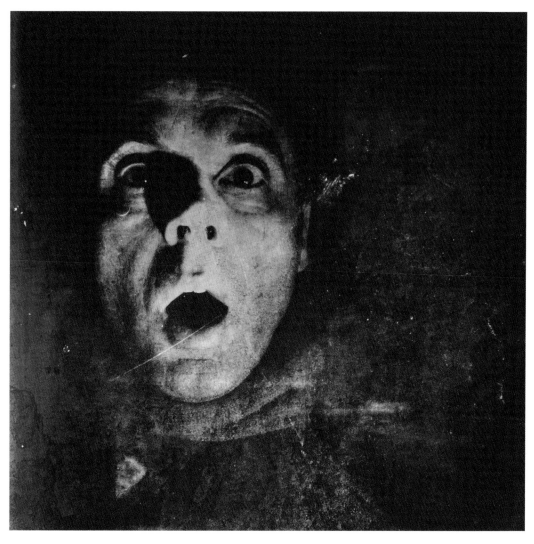

Silver Star launched a hasty rescue mission and located the ship, which at first sight appeared to be completely undamaged but when they went on board they discovered the entire crew had died, and all their faces were contorted with a look of sheer terror. According to the *Proceedings of the Merchant Marine Council* in 1952, the bodies were found "sprawled on their backs, the frozen faces upturned to the sun with mouths gaping open and eyes staring."

Above: With mouths agape and wide eyes staring, it was reported that "the dead bodies resembled horrible caricatures."

The captain was found on the bridge, while the officers' bodies were lying all over the wheelhouse and chartroom. The radio operator was found dead, still at his post, his eyes wide open, and with his fingers on the telegraph, having tapped out that final message. The crew of the *Silver Star* continued their search below deck, where they found more corpses in the boiler room, and even though the temperature outside was a sweltering 110°F (43°C), there was a strange chill in the hold that no one could explain.

There was no damage to the ship, no signs of injury to the corpses, nor any evidence of foul play. The captain of the *Silver Star* decided to tow the *Ourang Medan* back to port, but smoke soon began to billow from its lower decks, and the decision was made to cut the towline and abandon it. Fire took hold of the ship, causing an explosion that lifted it from the water, before it sank.

A SHIFTING TALE
The first reports of the demise of *Ourang Medan* were published in a Dutch-Indonesian newspaper between February and March 1948, written by the Italian author Silvio Scherli, but the name of

Above: The fate of the Dutch merchant ship is shrouded in mystery, and its very existence is questionable, although it is possible to find photographs that are claimed to be of the ship.

the *Silver Star* was never mentioned. The stories were based on the testimony of an unnamed German, who claimed to be the sole survivor of the *Ourang Medan* crew, and who was found by an Italian missionary and natives on the Taongi Atoll, a largely uninhabited coral atoll in the Marshall Islands. Before he died, the German sailor told the missionary that the ship had been traveling from an unnamed Chinese port to Costa Rica in secret and was carrying a supply of sulfuric acid, which leaked on board, killing the crew and sinking the ship.

The Italian missionary told this to Scherli, who wrote the stories for the newspaper, but they in turn published a disclaimer: "This is the last part of our story about the mystery of the *Ourang Medan*. We must repeat that we don't have any other data on this 'mystery of the sea.' Nor can we answer the many unanswered questions in the story. It may seem obvious that this is a thrilling romance of the sea. On the other hand, the author, Silvio Scherli, assures us of the authenticity of the story."

The problem with the whole incident is that there is no evidence that the *Ourang Medan* (which translates as "Man from Medan" in Indonesian) existed. Over the last 70 years, no one has managed to locate details of the ship's registration, history, or construction. Nothing at all. There is no mention of the ship in Lloyd's Register of Ships or in any country. While the *Silver Star* did exist, its logs have no record of its attempting to rescue the *Ourang Medan*, and in any case it was to be found sailing around Brazil rather than the Straits of Malacca, or anywhere near the Marshall Islands.

Crucially, no member of the *Silver Star* ever spoke about what they discovered when they boarded the *Ourang Medan*. No one came forward to substantiate the story of their rescue. To add to the mystery, reports of the sinking of the *Ourang Medan* can be traced back to November 1940, more than six years before it was supposed to have happened, according to Silvio Scherli.

The British newspapers the *Daily Mirror* and the *Yorkshire Post* had carried an Associated Press report containing many of the same details that would appear in 1948, but, crucially, there was no mention of the terrified look of the corpses, the SOS communication was different, and the ship was found in the Solomon Islands. The source was not a soon-to-perish survivor, but a merchant marine officer from the rescuing ship who was unnamed. There is also evidence that this version of the tale came from the same Silvio Scherli.

Among so many conflicting reports about the ship, there is nothing to suggest it ever existed, or that the *Silver Star* attempted to rescue it, but that has not stopped the story from enduring for all these years, with speculation about how the crew came to die on board.

Below: It is possible that the ship was on the fixed maritime shipping route mapped below.

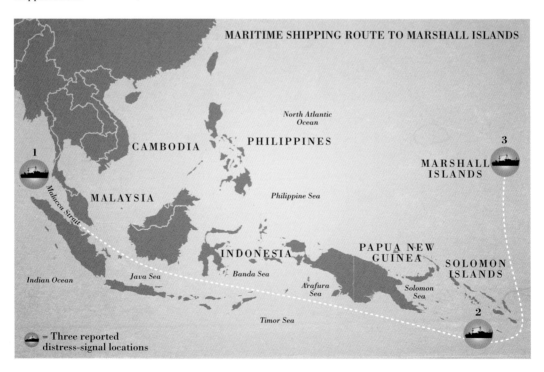

MARITIME SHIPPING ROUTE TO MARSHALL ISLANDS

1

CAMBODIA

PHILIPPINES

North Atlantic
Ocean

3

MARSHALL
ISLANDS

MALAYSIA

Philippine Sea

Malacca Strait

INDONESIA

PAPUA NEW
GUINEA

SOLOMON
ISLANDS

Indian Ocean

Java Sea

Banda Sea

*Arafura
Sea*

*Solomon
Sea*

Timor Sea

2

= Three reported
distress-signal locations

— ALTERNATIVE —
THEORIES

The most popular theory is that the *Ourang Medan* was involved in smuggling chemicals, including potassium cyanide, nitroglycerin, and nerve agents, from World War II. It is speculated that water got into the ship's hold and mixed with the chemicals to release a toxic gas that caused asphyxia and poisoning among the crew, leading to the fire and explosion that sank it. A more plausible theory is that a fire in the ship's boiler produced carbon monoxide that spread, fatally knocking out the whole crew. Could the crew have been killed by something outside the ship? An old seafaring tale claimed

Above: Was the ship smuggling chemicals when it exploded on the shipping route to the Marshall Islands?

that a methane bubble came up from a fissure on the seafloor and overwhelmed the ship, killing everyone on board with clouds of noxious methane. The alleged terrified looks on the faces of the dead has led others to speculate that they were attacked by a UFO in the middle of the ocean. These unexplained looks, the lack of natural causes for their deaths, and that strange chill in the cargo hold form the basis of this rather hollow theory.

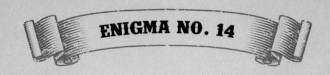

WERE THE LOST COSMONAUTS SACRIFICED FOR THE SPACE RACE?

Date: 1959–1976
Location: Outer space

Two superpowers embarked on a Space Race that would ultimately see man land on the Moon: both the Soviet Union and America competed for superiority on Earth and beyond, but at what cost?

In late July 1955, a decade after the end of World War II, America announced its intent to launch artificial satellites into orbit. The Soviet Union responded, and the Space Race was under starter's orders. In the struggle that followed to outdo their foe, both nations spent vast amounts of money in the quest for domination. There are those who believe that the Soviet Union covered up a series of tragic accidents and that many cosmonauts, in their country's rush to be the first to conquer space, paid the ultimate price. While the Soviet Union won the race to launch the first successful satellite into orbit with *Sputnik 1* in October 1957, it was not long before the rumors began to emerge.

LOST IN SPACE

In December 1959 it was alleged that a high-ranking Czech communist had leaked information about the death of Aleksei Ledovsky, killed during the launch of a converted R-5A rocket. Three other names—Andrei Mitkov, Sergei Shiborin, and Maria Gromova—were also later cited as losing their lives in similar circumstances. The Soviets denied claims that their cosmonauts were dying, but rumors persisted.

In 1960, author Robert Heinlein wrote that while traveling through what is today Lithuania, he was told by Red Army cadets that there had recently been an unsuccessful manned space launch. The *Korabl-Sputnik 1* had indeed been launched, before a mechanical fault with its guidance system sent it in the wrong direction. Soviet authorities' official line was that this was an unmanned test flight, but Heinlein was adamant that he had been told that this was a failed attempt to put man into space and that the cosmonaut on board had been lost.

Above: After the destruction of World War II, the United States and Russia embarked on a race to be seen as the most technologically advanced, the most innovative, and the most worthy of being called the planet's ultimate "superpower."

Above: A piece of the *Korabl-Sputnik 1* was apparently found in the middle of North 8th Street in Manitowoc, Wisconsin, in the northern United States.

STRANGE TRANSMISSIONS

Supporting this damning theory was the emergence of a number of radio transmissions picked up by two eager Italians. Achille and Giovanni Judica-Cordiglia were keen amateur radio operators who began to monitor Soviet space program transmissions in 1957 and claimed they had, on November 28, 1960, picked up an SOS transmission from the *Korabl-Sputnik 1* flight. The nature of the transmission suggested there was indeed a person on board and, due to an error, the satellite was heading deep into space. Was this actually the first manned flight into orbit?

The Judica-Cordiglia brothers continued to monitor Soviet transmissions, including one in which they claimed to have heard a woman's voice. She was speaking in Russian, but the message was soon translated, and she was found to be telling mission control she could see flames and she was fearful that her capsule was about to explode. The Soviets denied these transmissions. The brothers released nine recordings, all refuted by the Soviet authorities, but nevertheless pouring further doubt onto the transparency of its space program. One of their discoveries was in early April 1961, when they detected a signal from a capsule orbiting the Earth three times before re-entry.

Days later, on April 7, 1961, the Soviet Union claimed a great victory over the USA in the race for space travel, when they launched Yuri Gagarin into orbit in his Vostok spacecraft. Amid the celebrations, though, there were counterclaims that the capsule whose signal the Judica-Cordiglia brothers had picked up was that of a failed flight, manned by a Vladimir Ilyushin, who in fact was the first man in space but whose mission failed, meaning an emergency re-entry, and that he landed in China, where he was captured and kept prisoner for a year.

The Soviets rubbished these reports, stating there had been no failure and that the success of Gagarin was where their attention lay. They conceded that Ilyushin was indeed in China for a year but had been receiving treatment for an injury. Skeptics argued that the international embarrassment they would have felt from this failed attempt was symbolic of their other cover-ups.

Below: Was Vladimir Ilyushin the first man in space, before he crash-landed in China?

THE RACE FOR THE MOON

Ultimately, the United States won the race to the Moon, when, in July 1969, *Apollo 11* landed on the lunar surface, claiming a great Cold War victory. However, it is alleged that weeks before *Apollo*'s launch, the Soviets had attempted to send a manned Soyuz-7K-L3, launched via the powerful N1 rocket, to the Moon, but an explosion destroyed the launchpad and killed the cosmonauts on board.

Above: Buzz Aldrin with the Stars and Stripes on the Moon in the *Apollo 11* landing.

Soviet officials once again denied the allegations, arguing that the craft was never ready for manned missions and that the launch had only ever been a test for the rocket's booster. While their rivals successfully landed on the Moon, the Soviet manned program continued to be shrouded in mystery and in 1976 was disbanded without success. There are those who believe that the automated Soviet robotic lander missions to the Moon were, in fact, controlled by cosmonauts on one-way and ultimately deadly missions.

The Cold War may have ended in 1991 with the fall of the Soviet Union, but intrigue, rumor, and counter-rumor continue to fascinate, and when it comes to the Space Race and the case of Russia's lost cosmonauts, there remains a desire for one giant leap toward the truth.

ALTERNATIVE
THEORIES

Decades after the race for space started, plenty of declassified documents have been released, none of which contain evidence of lost cosmonauts. However, skeptics still believe that such was the depth of the Soviet cover-up, a lack of documented evidence is not enough to dispel their theories. Many who do not believe in the cover-up of cosmonaut fatalities point to the many publicized deaths, including the 1960 death of at least 78 ground crew when a rocket ignited on a launchpad. Then there was the 1967 death of a cosmonaut when the parachute on his space capsule failed to open.

Above: Yuri Gagarin went on to lose his life while training, a year after his famous mission.

In relation to the *Korabl-Sputnik 1* launch and Robert Heinlein's claims that it was indeed a manned mission that was lost in space, the Soviet authorities point to the vessel's lack of a re-entry shield, stating that the mission was never meant to return, and therefore could not have been manned.

Yuri Gagarin, the first official man in space, stated in his autobiography that the theories about his country's lost men and women were all explained by accidents that occurred in low orbit and not in space. There are plenty, though, who are unconvinced.

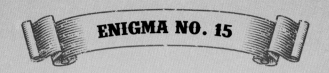
DID VALENTICH ENCOUNTER UFOS?

Date: October 1978
Location: Bass Strait, Australia

A young Australian pilot reports that he is being followed by an unidentified object in the air—within minutes, he disappears, never to be seen or heard from again.

On the evening of October 21, 1978, Frederick Valentich set off from Moorabbin airport in Victoria, piloting a Cessna 182 light aircraft for a 125-mile (200-kilometer) flight to King Island, across the Bass Strait, which separates the Australian mainland and Tasmania. Just over 45 minutes into his flight, the young pilot radioed Melbourne air traffic control to report that an unidentified aircraft was following him, only to be told by controller Steve Robey there was nothing in that area. Valentich was convinced, "It [has] four bright [lights], it seems to me like landing lights … The aircraft has just passed over me at least a thousand feet above. It's approaching right now from due east toward me … It seems to me that he's playing some sort of game. He's flying over me two, three times, at a time at speeds I could not identify."

Above: Valentich was a 20-year-old Australian shop assistant with an interest in aviation, a fascination with UFOs, and a class-four instrument rating, which allowed him to fly at night.

Valentich also reported that he was having difficulty controlling the aircraft and that the engine was beginning to choke and rough-ride. After six minutes of being in radio contact, with Valentich growing ever more agitated, his final words were: "That strange aircraft is hovering on top of me again … It is hovering, and it's not an aircraft." There then follows 17 seconds of a strange metallic scraping sound, before all contact is lost.

THE SEARCH FOR VALENTICH

A sea and air search was immediately launched, while all other ships and planes in the area were asked to look out for Valentich's aircraft and any signs of wreckage. An oil slick north of King Island was discovered the next day, but there was no connection to Valentich's aircraft and, after four days, the search was called off.

In May 1982 the Bureau of Air Safety reported that the reasons for Valentich's disappearance had not been determined; however, it was "presumed fatal." A year later, an engine cowl flap from a Cessna 182 aircraft was found washed ashore on Flinders Island, which featured a serial number from a range that included Valentich's aircraft.

Valentich was an inexperienced pilot, who had twice applied to join the Royal Australian Air Force, but had been rejected. At the time of his disappearance, he was studying to be a commercial pilot, but had failed all five license exams. He had been reprimanded by the aviation authorities for straying into a controlled zone in Sydney, and for deliberately flying into a cloud.

The reason for Valentich's flight to King Island has never been properly established: he had said he was headed there to collect friends, but there were none waiting for him; he also said he went there for crayfish, but there is no record of him having ordered any. His father, Guido, spoke about his son's obsession with UFOs—how he claimed to have seen one and how he feared being abducted by one, which has led to a strong belief that he made the flight to look for UFOs. "The fact that they have no trace of him really verifies the fact that UFOs could have been there," his father said in the days that followed his son's disappearance.

In 2004 researcher Keith Basterfield discovered the official file on Valentich's disappearance in the online National Archives index, even though he had been told it was lost or destroyed. But the 315-page file provides few clues or answers. "The only thing we can say for sure is that the plane and pilot disappeared while he was describing a UFO, which is one of those things that just makes people wonder," Basterfield told the *Adelaide Advertiser*.

A 2013 study by the astronomer and retired US Air Force pilot James McGaha and author Joe Nickell concluded that the inexperienced pilot had lost control of the plane by seeing a tilted horizon and, in attempting to compensate, put the plane into what is known as a "graveyard spiral," which sent it into Bass Strait. The report also stated that the tightening spiral of the plane would have limited fuel flow, causing the rough riding Valentich had reported to air traffic control. And the bright lights that Valentich saw above him? McGaha and Nickell believe they were simply the planets Mars, Venus, and Mercury, and the star Antares. There has been further speculation that a disorientated Valentich was flying upside down, and that the lights were reflections of his own.

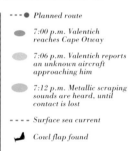

- - - ● Planned route

    7:00 p.m. Valentich reaches Cape Otway

    7:06 p.m. Valentich reports an unknown aircraft approaching him

    7:12 p.m. Metallic scraping sounds are heard, until contact is lost

- - - - Surface sea current

    Cowl flap found

Above: It is likely that a disorientated Valentich, flying from Moorabbin to King Island, lost control of the plane and crashed into the ocean, with Bass Strait's strong currents taking the light aircraft a long distance before it sank.

— ALTERNATIVE —
THEORIES

UFO enthusiasts claim that Valentich's disappearance was caused by the presence of an alien aircraft. Ground Saucer Watch, an organization based in Phoenix, Arizona, has said there were reports of green lights in the sky over Bass Strait on the evening of October 21. They also point to photographs taken by Roy Manifold, a plumber and amateur photographer who set up a time-lapse camera on a tripod on the shoreline to capture the sun setting over the water. A photograph shows a fast-moving object, estimated to be traveling at 200 mph (320 km/hour), exiting the water near the Cape Otway lighthouse 20 minutes before Valentich reported he was having difficulties. However, the picture is not clear enough to identify the object, and there is no strong evidence that it was a UFO.

Could Valentich have staged his own disappearance? He had enough fuel to travel for 500 miles (800 km), and Melbourne police did receive reports that a light aircraft had made a landing not far from Cape Otway that same evening. Basterfield says that the official report contains no suggestion it was a hoax. Suicide was also ruled out as a theory after doctors, friends, and colleagues spoke about Valentich as a content and well-adjusted young man.

Below: Where did the Cessna 182 end up, and why?

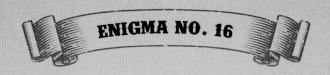
WHERE DID SHERGAR DISAPPEAR TO?

Date: February 8, 1983
Location: County Kildare, Ireland

In the early eighties, the Irish horse Shergar was revered as the most valuable and brilliant racehorse in the world. Then, one cold and foggy night, this amazing horse was forcibly taken from his stud farm, never to be seen again…

During its short career, the bay colt with the distinctive white blaze competed in only eight races, winning six of them, including the Derby— with the largest margin in the race's 202-year history—the Irish Derby, and the King George VI stakes. In October 1981 Shergar was retired to stud by his owner, the Aga Khan, a billionaire spiritual leader to 15 million Ismaili Muslims. The Aga Khan sold 34 shares for £250,000 each to create a syndicate, which would charge racehorse owners as much as £80,000 for Shergar's services as a breeding stallion. In 1982 Shergar impregnated 35 mares, and for the following year was set to do the same to 55 more at the Ballymany stud farm near the Curragh racecourse in County Kildare.

MASKED GANG

On February 8, 1983, on a cold and foggy evening, a gang of between six and nine men wearing balaclavas, and carrying guns, arrived at the farm in three vehicles, with one pulling a horsebox.

Shortly after 8:30 p.m., three of the gang knocked on the front door of Shergar's head groom, Jim Fitzgerald. The door was answered by his eldest son, Bernard, who was struck, before Fitzgerald himself had a pistol pointed at him. "We have come for Shergar, we want £2 million," he was told. Two members of the gang guarded Fitzgerald's wife, Madge, and their five children, while at gunpoint Fitzgerald took the rest of the gang to Shergar's stable and helped load the horse into the horsebox.

Above: Shergar in all his glory, winning the Derby at Epsom by 10 lengths on June 3, 1981, with jockey Walter Swinburn on his back.

It is not known where Shergar was taken, but Fitzgerald was placed in a separate vehicle and driven around for three hours before being given a code ("King Neptune"), to be used in negotiations, and then dumped by the side of the road. Fitzgerald found a phone box and first alerted the stud manager Ghislain Drion that Shergar had been kidnapped, before phoning his brother for a lift home, where he discovered his family had been unharmed.

POLICE INVOLVEMENT

However, incredibly, the police were not informed of Shergar's disappearance for another five hours, which was a full eight hours after he had been taken, by which time the horse could have been taken out of Ireland.

The police response was botched from the beginning, with them even turning to mediums and psychics to learn of Shergar's whereabouts, and at one point in the investigation, the police chief superintendent James "Spud" Murphy was candid enough to admit, "Clues? Oh, now, that's something we don't have." The investigation was also hampered by Shergar being taken the day before Ireland's biggest racehorse sale, so the roads were covered with horseboxes when they were out searching for one, while officers from both Dublin and County Kildare were assigned to the case, but refused to share information with each other.

Twenty-four hours after Shergar's disappearance, an anonymous call was made to the BBC newsroom in Belfast, stating that the kidnappers would only negotiate with three horseracing journalists: Lord Oaksey from the *Daily Telegraph*, Peter Campling from the *Sun*, and Derek Thompson from ITV. The next day the trio flew to Belfast before making their way to a farm owned by horse breeder Jeremy Maxwell, 30 miles (50 kilometers) from Belfast, where they fielded between 10 and 12 calls from the kidnappers throughout the night. At first the kidnappers made a

Above: A Garda (Irish police) officer stands on duty in the grounds of the Ballymany stud farm, from where Shergar was taken.

demand for an initial payment of £40,000, while Thompson asked for a picture of Shergar alongside a copy of a newspaper from that day, but nothing could be agreed. All communication went dead for six hours, until the kidnappers phoned for a final time at 6:55 a.m. and said, "The horse has had an accident. He's dead."

Meanwhile, for the next three days, other kidnappers were negotiating directly with a representative of the Aga Khan, who never countenanced paying a ransom, for it would forever make him and his syndicate vulnerable to further extortion. All communication with the kidnappers ceased, but the police search continued for several weeks, without gaining any meaningful leads.

WHO TOOK SHERGAR?

The identity of the kidnappers remains unknown to this day, but the main suspects have always been the Provisional IRA. In 1999 a former IRA operative-turned-informant, Sean O'Callaghan, published the book *The Informer,* in which he claimed to know the details behind Shergar's disappearance. "[An IRA] cell thought: 'Why not kidnap Shergar?' The horse had no family. They were convinced that the Aga Khan would pay up. It couldn't go wrong. This was going to be a quick way to make money, very quick," O'Callaghan said. "But, if they had thought about it, they would have realized paying a ransom would have left the Aga Khan open to all kinds of extortion threats. The money was a non-starter."

When it dawned on the gang that they would not be able to profit from stealing the horse, they believed they had no option but to kill it, especially after it had apparently injured its leg. "One of the gang suggested to me that Shergar was killed within hours [of being taken]," says O'Callaghan. "Shot dead. He went demented in the horsebox and badly injured his leg. They had to kill him because they couldn't call a vet, they had the most recognizable horse in the world on their hands. [It was a] total cock-up from start to finish." Derek Thompson lends credence to O'Callaghan's story as he was given a password in his negotiations with the kidnappers, which he never shared with anyone, but that the former IRA man uses in his book.

The Irish police chief Sean Feely took over the investigation in 1995, and stated that another informant told him that the horse's body was buried in woodland at Ballinamore in County Leitrim, in the north of Ireland. The case file remains open.

Below: Chief Superintendent James Murphy gives details of three of the suspected "horsenappers" to the international press.

—ALTERNATIVE—
THEORIES

Walter Swinburn, the jockey who rode Shergar to victory in the 1981 Derby, has said: "I have heard a million and one theories [about what happened]." The most compelling theory has always been that the IRA stole the horse to secure a large ransom from the Aga Khan to raise funds for the paramilitary organization, but when the money didn't materialize they were forced to kill the horse. It has also been suggested that the IRA stole Shergar for the Libyan dictator Colonel Gaddafi in return for a cache of weapons. Another more far-fetched theory was that the New Orleans Mafia had taken Shergar. The French bloodstock dealer Jean Michel Gambet borrowed money from the Mafia to buy a horse from the Aga Khan, but the deal collapsed and the money was lost by Gambet, who would later be found dead, shot in the head in a car in Kentucky. The Mafia believed they were owed a horse, and so took Shergar. Maybe…

Above: Did the Aga Khan, here in the top hat and to the left of the horse, leading Shergar after winning the Derby, refuse to pay an IRA ransom?

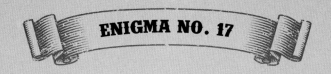

WHAT BECAME OF RICHEY EDWARDS?

Date: February 1, 1995
Location: London, England

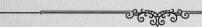

The troubled and beloved Manic Street Preachers guitarist fled from a London hotel early one morning and was never seen again.

At the start of 1995, Richey Edwards was a guitarist with the hugely successful Manic Street Preachers, and was hailed as one of the greatest songwriters of his generation, following the release of their critically acclaimed album *The Holy Bible*. Edwards was a tortured soul, not fully able to enjoy being in this increasingly popular rock band. He suffered from alcoholism, anorexia, and depression. He also confessed a deep desire to self-harm: "When I cut myself, I feel so much better. All the little things that might have been annoying me suddenly seem so trivial because I'm concentrating on the pain. I'm not a person who can scream and shout, so this is my only outlet." In May 1991, on stage at a concert in Norwich, UK, he even carved "4Real" into his arm with a razor, as a message to those who questioned his musical credibility, and at a 1994 concert in Thailand he gashed his chest with a knife.

At the start of 1995, it was hoped Edwards, who had turned 27 the previous month, was beginning to be able to control his excesses, and had started to rehearse for their fourth album and a forthcoming tour of the United States. On January 31, Edwards checked into the Embassy Hotel in London with his bandmate James Dean Bradfield, ahead of the pair catching a flight to the US for a promotional tour the next day. In a telephone call with his mother, Edwards said he was not looking forward to traveling to the US. At approximately 7 a.m. the next morning, Edwards checked out of the hotel, taking his wallet, car keys, passport, and some Prozac, but leaving behind his packed suitcase. Edwards drove to his apartment in the Welsh capital Cardiff—some reports say it took him eight hours to get there, at least double the expected time—where he left his wallet, passport, and the Prozac, and slipped away, never to be seen again.

Above: The Manic Street Preachers on stage at the Zap Club, Brighton, UK, in 1991. Four years later, a US tour was in the pipeline, but so was Richey's (on the left) disappearance.

Above: Richey's car—lived in and locked up—was found abandoned at the service station next to the Severn Bridge.

In the following two weeks, there were reports Edwards had been seen by a fan, David Cross, at Newport bus station, and a fan who was unaware he was supposed to be missing claimed to have had a conversation with him at Newport passport office. On February 7, Newport taxi driver Anthony Hatherhall picked up a person he believed to be Edwards from the King's Hotel in the town, and drove him around the valleys, including where Edwards grew up in Blackwood. Hatherhall recalled that the man he believed to be Edwards acted strangely—he had a lie down on the back seat—and when engaged in conversation, his accent slipped between his native Welsh and an exaggerated cockney. The passenger was eventually dropped off at the Severn View service station near Aust, South Gloucestershire, next to the Severn Bridge, before settling his fare of £68 in cash.

GLIMMERS OF HOPE

A week later, February 14, Edwards' silver Vauxhall Cavalier received a parking ticket, and three days later the police discovered the car had been abandoned at the same service station next to the Severn Bridge. The car had a flat battery, but there were obvious signs someone had lived in the car for several days, including some discarded burger wrappers. A lock had been attached to the steering wheel, which gave Edwards' family a glimmer of hope. As his sister Rachel Elias has said in later years, "Why would you worry about someone stealing your car if you were chaotically thinking of ending your life?" The discovery of his car next to the

Below: The Severn Bridge is a known suicide spot, but strong tides in the water below often carry bodies out to sea, meaning they are never found.

Above: Richey's sister, Rachel Elias, does not believe Richey jumped, and continues the search.

Severn Bridge, a spot where many others had committed suicide in the past, made many draw the obvious conclusion that he, too, had taken his own life there in the days after he fled London.

Expecting Richey to eventually follow on, James Dean Bradfield had traveled to the US on February 1, but once it became clear Edwards had disappeared, the band stopped recording and touring for the rest of the year, as the search continued. However, the trail went cold, and Richey's body has never been found. There has been a succession of credible sightings of him, though, in the years since. Toward the end of 1996, college lecturer Vyvyan Morris, who was on holiday in a resort in Goa, believes she spotted Richey in a local market, briefly spoke to him, and learned he was now going by the name of Rick.

In 1998, in the Underground bar on the Canary Island of Fuerteventura, customers believed that a man at the bar could be Edwards. Speaking at the time, British barmaid Tracey Jones said: "One of the customers suddenly shouted, 'You're Richey from the Manic Street Preachers!' He just started to run toward the door and within seconds he had gone. We were sure he was just like Richey." It was enough to lure his parents, Graham and Sherry, to Fuerteventura, but the trail went cold once again, and there were no further sightings on the island. In 2008, six years after it was first possible, his parents were granted a court order for their son to be declared dead.

— ALTERNATIVE —
THEORIES

The leading theory is that soon after abandoning his car at the service station next to the Severn Bridge, Edwards threw himself off it and committed suicide. A body was never found in the water below, however, and his friends and family have long disputed he would have ended his own life. The year before he disappeared, Edwards himself, despite his many struggles, ruled out this possibility. "In terms of the 'S' word, that does not enter my mind, and it never has done, in terms of an attempt. Because I am stronger than that. I might be a weak person, but I can take pain."

Above: Did Richey fake his death to escape stardom and find paradise in Fuerteventura?

So where is Edwards? In the two weeks before his disappearance, he had withdrawn £200 a day for 14 consecutive days to raise a total of £2,800. Did he use the money to start a new life? The possible sightings of him abroad, including in Fuerteventura, add weight to this theory.

In the years since he disappeared, his bandmate Nicky Wire has said, "Personally, I still think he's alive, although I've got no physical evidence or reason to think that he is. But I do… How can you accept that he's dead, when there's no body, no evidence whatsoever? It's irrational."

THE SUPERNATURAL

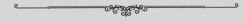

Is there something under the bed? Do old houses merely creak in the wind or... ? From childhood, notions of things beyond our realms of reality have us wanting to know more—while closing our eyes and hoping that the noise will go away. This chapter takes us back to sitting around the campfire to learn more about stories of ghostly encounters, possessed houses, and unexplained supernatural phenomena.

Why did so many seemingly rational people testify to seeing what they perceived as the haunting of an otherwise normal suburban home in London? How can the strange faces that appeared on the floor of a small Spanish home in the small village of Bélmez be explained away as merely a hoax, when so much scientific evidence suggests that there was no way anyone could have mocked up the eerie faces? And then there's Don Decker, or "Rain Man," as he became infamously known. Why and how did this young man seemingly make it rain indoors? Was this once again an elaborate hoax, or evidence of paranormal powers, perhaps brought on by a deep psychological trauma and, therefore, a sign that there is so much more to learn about the human psyche?

By studying cases like these, it becomes clear that there is still much to learn about what we perceive to be natural and supernatural.

Left: Why and how did water spontaneously spring from ceilings and walls when the Rain Man was around?

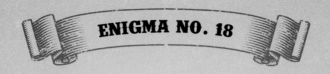
WHAT CAUSES THE MARFA GHOST LIGHTS?

Date: 1883–Present day
Location: Marfa, Texas

Strange orbs of light have been seen floating around the Texan night sky, outside a small town called Marfa. Many have theories, but no one can explain the Marfa Ghost Lights...

On a winter's night in 1883, not long after sunset, young cowhand Robert Reed Ellison sat out on the plains through which he was driving his cattle. He'd made himself something to eat, checked on his animals, and was ready to settle down for the night. He was out near a small settlement called Marfa, just west of Paisano Pass. Looking out into the darkness, a light caught his eye. At first, he feared Apache signal fires and, worried for his herd's safety, he took to his horse and searched the surrounding countryside. He found no one and no manmade fires. The sun came up, and all Ellison could think of was what he had seen.

Confused and a little scared, the young man went to the settlers in Marfa and told them what he had seen: little orbs of light in the distance, seemingly dancing in the night sky. Some of those he told raised an eyebrow and laughed off his sightings. Others listened and said they had seen the same thing before. The mystery of the Marfa Ghost Lights had begun, and it hasn't gone away.

Above: This supernatural enigma began with a young cowhand who found himself out on the plains, witnessing strange, dancing orbs of light.

THE LEGEND GROWS

From those days of the early settlers driving cattle, the legend of the ghostly lights grew faster than the town of Marfa itself. In 1956 the Hollywood blockbuster *Giant* was filmed on the dusty plains that surround the town and it is said that its main star, James Dean, arrived fixated on the lights, bringing a telescope with him to the hotel and, when not falling for Elizabeth Taylor

on set, would scan the night sky, hoping to catch a glimpse.
Dean must have heard about the strange lights through word
of mouth, but a year after *Giant* was released, the first account
of the sightings was published in the July 1957 issue of *Coronet*,
a popular general digest magazine. As Americans read about this
peculiar story, more experiences of the lights were reported and
soon, with the advent of travel, tourists came from farther afield.

In 1976 the author Elton Miles wrote *Tales of the Big Bend*,
a collection of Texan folklore stories that prominently included
eyewitness accounts of the lights, plus an old photograph
claiming to catch the phenomenon. Miles's book, along with
the continuance of sightings and fascinating photographs,
slowly built a legend.

Below: Legendary star
of *Giant*, James Dean,
was determined to spot
the lights while filming
out on the Marfa plains.

MARFA WELCOMES THE WORLD

In 2003, such was the global interest,
a viewing platform was erected out on
a half-moon-shaped area adjoining
Highway 67. People come from all over
the world to stare across the Chinati
Mountains, and it is said that on about
30 occasions a year, in different seasons,
people leave saying they have seen the
mysterious orbs and have photographs.
Witnesses talk of round lights the size of
basketballs darting across the night sky,
pulsating as they go. Other accounts report
colored spheres twinkling in the distance.
Colors vary: sometimes yellow; sometimes
blue, red, or white. Sometimes they dart
wildly across the sky; sometimes they just
float; sometimes they merge into one.

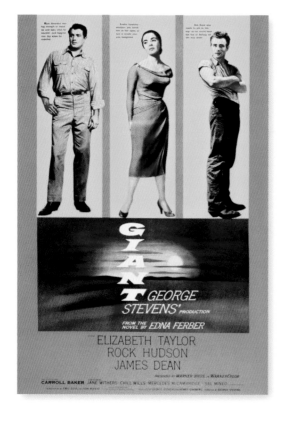

Above: Such is the popularity of the lights, there is a devoted viewing platform, which has been host to around 30 reported sightings a year.

"I've been to far West Texas a dozen times over the past decade, so of course I've seen the lights, as people have for more than a century," said Michael Hall, a keen believer. "I've seen them at dusk and at midnight, in the summer and the fall, by myself and with other people. They appeared in the darkness south of US 90, between Alpine and Marfa: yellowish-white lights that glowed, faded, disappeared, and returned in different places. Sometimes they changed colors, other times they split apart. I couldn't tell if they were 10 miles away or a hundred, the size of a car or a house. I didn't understand them, but I didn't care. I loved those lights."

Marfa, an arty but quintessentially Texan town, has certainly gained outside recognition from the legend of its lights, but it is local James Bunnell, a former NASA aerospace engineer who attended Marfa High School, who has studied the phenomenon more than any other. In 2000, having returned to his hometown, Bunnell witnessed for himself the lights over the desert, calling them, "A shocking display, for which I could find no explanation." For over a decade he investigated; like so many others, though, he couldn't fathom any pattern or concrete reasons as to why the lights would emerge. He did conclude that there had been 34 sightings of the lights between 1945 and 2008, but was adamant that plenty were missed as tourists are limited to just the viewing stations.

"You might just see mysterious orbs of light suddenly appear above desert foliage," Bunnell explained. "These balls of light may remain stationary as they pulse on and off with intensity varying from dim to almost blinding brilliance. Then again, these ghostly lights may dart across the desert … or perform splits and mergers. Marfa Mystery Lights usually fly above desert vegetation but below background mesas."

Below: Local Bunnell states, "light colors are usually yellow-orange, but other hues, including green, blue, and red, are also seen."

— ALTERNATIVE — THEORIES

A hoax to attract tourists is a possible but perhaps simplistic explanation. Many looking for an easy answer suggest the lights are nothing but car lights moving along nearby Highway 90. As for the hovering quality the lights give off, helicopter lights or border control low-flying aircraft have been suggested. Yet that wouldn't explain Robert Reed Ellison's story in 1883. One skeptic has mentioned a mirage caused by sharp temperature gradients between cold and warm layers of air, arguing that Marfa's location at nearly 5,000 feet (1,500 meters) and the often varying temperatures might be causing the illusion of floating light.

In May 2008 scientists from Texas University studying the interaction of electromagnetic radiation (spectroscopy) set up equipment that observed the phenomenon for 20 days, but their findings were inconclusive, saying they did see lights but they could have been distant fires or, indeed, cars.

Above: There are plenty who, when studying the Marfa Lights, point to the notoriety the lights have afforded the place and dismiss them as a hoax.

As for the residents of Marfa, even those who have never seen the lights cherish their legend and hold them very much as their own. "My parents and grandparents saw the lights," says Aurie West, whose family settled in Marfa in the 1880s. "They've always been here. I hope they never find out what's out there. Mysteries make life interesting."

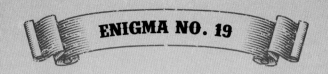

WHO IS HAUNTING BRISBANE CITY HALL?

Date: 1930–Present day
Location: Brisbane, Queensland, Australia

A beautiful civic building in a historic Australian city remains among the most haunted in the country. For decades, visitors and council workers have spoken of ghostly sightings, but who—or what—is responsible for the hauntings?

Over the years, Brisbane City Hall—the one-time tallest building in Queensland's capital—has been a proud structure in the city, a historic hub, but one which for many holds a darker side. The site of death and suicide, the hall is said by many residents of the city to be much more than their home's civic center—it's also a haunted building.

On October 31, 1935, all eyes were on the building's clocktower—but not to admire its beautiful architecture. A man was falling from the viewing tower. It was written in rather macabre fashion that the poor man "rudely disturbed the employees throughout the building" when he fell to his death. In the 1940s, a council worker committed suicide, jumping from a third-floor window and adding

to the growing list of horrific moments witnessed in the fairly new building. In that same decade a World War II veteran had got into a fight over a young lady with another serviceman and had been stabbed to death in the building's tea room.

A TRAGIC DEATH

However, it is the events of December 21, 1937, that led some to believe the building to be haunted. From the vibrant Christmas streets, policewoman Eileen O'Donnell spotted a crowd gathered below the clocktower. As O'Donnell got closer and followed the gaze of the crowd, she was shocked to see, up on the viewing tower, beyond the safety netting, a young lady standing on the ledge and edging herself around the platform. The police officer hoped to raise the alarm and possibly talk the lady down from danger. She was too late. To her horror, and to that of the now huge crowds that had gathered, the lady jumped. The noise she made as she crashed onto and through the City Hall roof, landing on a concrete floor, would stay in the memories of those unfortunate enough to be present. O'Donnell joined other officers and ambulance staff on the roof and discovered the badly injured lady, who turned out to be one Hilda Angus Boardman. She was still alive, but had a fractured skull and puncture wounds to her left side.

The medics stabilized Boardman and managed to get her to a hospital, but after only a couple of hours she was declared dead. In a short time, information regarding her identity emerged, as did the fact that she had been an inmate in a private institution, suggesting that she had suffered from a long-term mental illness. She left behind a husband and two children.

THE HAUNTING OF THE HALL

It was in the late 1930s and into the 1940s that people first started to talk of ghostly sightings within the building. In 1944 another lady had died there: Miriam Mary Alexander, a 55-year-old spinster on a visit to City Hall, complained of feeling ill and collapsed in its restrooms. There were also findings of drownings on the sight on which the building was built. Once a water hole, it is said that early residents of Brisbane fell victim to the pool's deep depths.

Above: Days after her fatal fall, Hilda Boardman was buried in a single grave plot in the far corner of the nearby Toowong Cemetery, soon to be joined by another "hall victim," Miriam Alexander.

Sightings of male ghosts have been reported, most notably a shadowy figure in the clocktower itself. This ghost has been nicknamed "Liftman," with a local paper, the *Queensland Independent*, writing that the "ghost has been continually riding the elevator since the 1930s," while the *City News* wrote in 2008 of "a maintenance man who rides the elevators who is rumored to have died in a freak accident." The most prominent and frequent sighting is that of a lady, elegant in her appearance, but her apparent age differs. Council workers over the decades have talked of strange footsteps, terrifying noises, and a female presence.

In 2012 a photograph of the building's foyer staircase emerged, showing an almost translucent figure of a woman dressed in a cloak descending the staircase. Today, the building's dark past and continued ghostly sightings make it among Brisbane's most famous and infamous locations.

— ALTERNATIVE —
THEORIES

Those who believe in the hauntings in Brisbane's City Hall have looked to the history of the city. The fact that the building was built on a spot where historical drownings took place many years before that first stone was laid interests some, but skeptics even within the supernatural community have their doubts that spirits of those who drowned long before the building was built, and with no connection to it, would ever return to haunt it.

The tragic deaths of Hilda Boardman and Miriam Alexander are events that interest believers far more, pointing specifically to the fact that Boardman was found—life draining out of her body—on the concrete floor of a small room just off the foyer that is now haunted. Another coincidence, this time focusing on the story of the Liftman, is a death that occurred in 1935. George Betts was visiting the tower on Halloween that year. The elevator had taken fellow visitors to the ground

Above: Strange noises and a female presence are usually heard and seen on the foyer stairs, and the mezzanine-level balcony overlooking the foyer.

floor, leaving Betts alone. Moments later, a loud crash was heard, and the body of George Betts was discovered down below. Is the ghost known as the Liftman this poor soul?

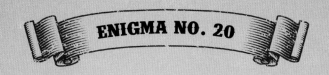

WHO—OR WHAT—WERE THE FACES OF BELMEZ?

Date: 1971–Present day
Location: Bélmez de la Moraleda, Andalusia, Spain

When face-like images appeared in the home of an Andalusian family, a whole nation became enthralled by the mystery. Were they an elaborate hoax, or signs of real paranormal activity?

On a hot August day in 1971, María Gómez Pereira was in her kitchen when she noticed something strange on the concrete floor. At first, she thought it was just a stain, fluid seeping up from below the slabs, perhaps, and she made a note to clean it later. Soon, though, Maria realized that the image left was that of a face. Not only that, it had moved.

Disturbed by the eerie human image looking up at her, María tried to scrub the stain out, but however hard she scrubbed and however hard she washed, the face remained—a bearded gentleman with piercing eyes staring up at her. María's husband, Juan, and her son, Miguel, decided to take a pickax to the slab and remove it before replacing the whole floor. Pleased to have seen the back of the image in their kitchen, the family were once again shocked when the face—the same bearded man—returned to the floor. Then it was joined by another, and another. The same man, the same face.

What had first appeared to be a coincidental, if very spooky, stain in their kitchen had turned into something haunting, and, as word spread, the population of their small town were very aware of what was happening in María's home.

HOUSE OF FACES

It wasn't long before the Pereira house was inundated with curious visitors, followed by the mayor of the town himself, interested to see what could be causing such a phenomenon at "The House of Faces." Within a year, people from all over Spain and even farther afield would come, excited by the prospect of this apparently haunted house.

Above: As the face apparitions intensified, they were sometimes a man, sometimes a woman, children too— sometimes clear, sometimes obscure, and in different parts of the house.

While their home became a tourist attraction, María was still constantly disturbed by the faces living with them. The family asked for the floor to be removed completely once again and that this time, experts in the field of parapsychology study the room and the house. It is these experts who claimed to have recorded "psychophonies," the name given within some spiritualist traditions to the phenomenon of spirits communicating through mediums. With the floor removed, the Pereiras agreed to a full excavation below the kitchen. It was then, while digging, that they found what many believers presumed to be the source of the faces.

HEADLESS SKELETONS

Ten feet (3 meters) below the surface were several skeletons. Thought to be 700 years old, a few of the skeletons were headless, prompting many to speculate that this was the reason for the appearance of faces. The skeletons were removed and given a proper burial at a nearby cemetery. With the surface filled in and the floor once again concreted over, it was only two weeks before an image returned, this time of a different face, then another. A face would appear in the morning and, by the evening, a new one had replaced it. The supposed haunting of the Pereira home had apparently intensified.

Journalists, students, and experts continued to try to solve the mystery, while skeptics tried to refute it. Dr. Hans Bender, a leading expert in the subject of parapsychology, traveled to Andalusia to study the strange events, and was immediately struck by what he found: "This is the most important paranormal case of the century," he stated. Dr. Bender advocated an "animistic" approach to parapsychology rather than a spiritualistic one, meaning that such phenomena were often seen by him as influenced not by the spirit world but by what he called the "focus person." In this case, that was María.

Tests continued to be carried out as faces continued to appear. There were always whispers of a hoax, whispers that grew louder, with many thinking this was all a plan hatched by María's son, to make money. One test, though, challenged that theory. For three months, the kitchen floor was covered and the kitchen sealed off from anyone. Under 24-hour surveillance and chronicled by a German television crew and several witnesses, no one got to the room or the floor, but, when with an audience the covers were lifted, new faces had once again appeared.

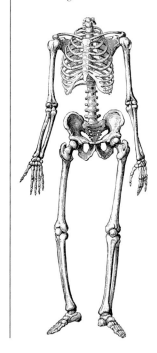

Below: The Pereiras hoped that the hauntings would be buried with the headless skeletons. They were wrong.

— ALTERNATIVE —
THEORIES

Soon after the first reappearance of these strange faces, the mayor of Bélmez de la Moraleda asked that one of the slabs be taken away to a lab for analysis. The tests proved inconclusive, and while many further tests pointed to the images being forged using paint, plenty of other expert analysts suggested that their origin simply couldn't be explained. After María's death in 2004, psychic researcher Pedro Amoros visited the house and claimed to have found new faces, but the local paper *El Mundo* discredited him by saying that his findings had been fake and, furthermore, he had connections to the municipal government and the whole thing had been a hoax concocted by both to attract fascinated tourists. Dr. Bender's theories around the focus person were in line with many who thought that it was María herself who had caused the images. Not purposefully, but through Thoughtography, the psychokinetic ability to project an image onto any surface, either deliberately or

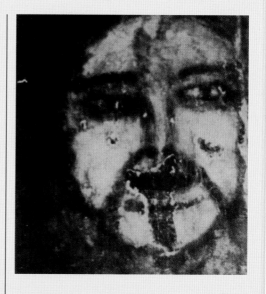

Above: Many academics who spent time with the family noted that the expressions on the faces resembled those on María's face at the time of their arrival.

unintentionally. The fact that faces have been reported since María's death, although less frequently than when she was alive and living in the house, only adds to the enigma that is the Faces of Bélmez.

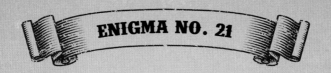

WAS THE ENFIELD HOUSE HAUNTED?

Date: 1977–1979
Location: London, England

On a warm summer's evening, Peggy Hodgson phoned the police with a strange complaint. In her daughters' shared room, furniture was moving around and noises were emanating from her walls. That was just the start…

Peggy Hodgson was separated from her partner and lived with her four children—two daughters, Margaret, aged 14, and Janet, 11; and two sons, Johnny, 10, and Billy, 7. Their home at 284 Green Street was on a terraced street in Enfield, on the northern outskirts of London, and was like so many other houses in suburban England. Theirs was a seemingly uneventful life. Peggy worked hard, the kids went to the local school. They knew their neighbors well and were popular members of the community. On the night of August 30, 1977, however, their lives were turned upside down, with unexplained events in their home that would haunt and terrify in equal measure.

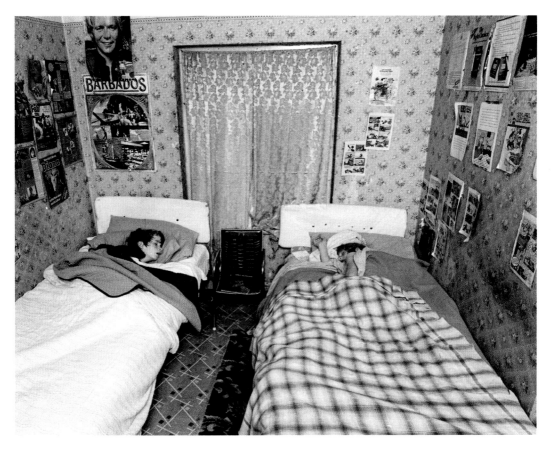

Above: The children's bedroom, seen here in 1977, was where many of the events were reported to have happened.

That night, having gotten her children to bed, Peggy was angered by noises coming from her daughters' room. She shouted up, and Janet replied worriedly that the bed was wobbling. Frustrated, Peggy ignored the strange claims and told them all to go to sleep. They did. The following night, it happened again. From downstairs, Peggy heard a crash. This time, she marched upstairs to tell the kids to stop playing around and get to sleep. On entering the room, a chest of drawers moved toward her. She moved it back but it resisted, and moved quickly toward her, as if wanting her out of the room. Was someone or something trying to keep her out? Noises started to be heard—noises they couldn't fathom. Terrified, the family put on their bathrobes, left the house, and knocked on their neighbors' door.

Vic and Margaret Nottingham were friendly with the family and listened intently to what they said. Vic settled them down and said he would have a look. "I went in there and I couldn't make out these noises," he later said. "There was a knocking on the wall, in the bedroom, on the ceiling. I was beginning to get a bit frightened." If a big burly builder was getting scared, they all thought it was time to call the police. Soon, PC Carolyn Heeps came by and, while skeptical, she herself spoke of a moving armchair, this time downstairs. Unsure of how the police could help, the officer left, and the family were once again alone. Perhaps the press could stir up some help. The *Daily Mirror* sent photographer Graham Morris, who witnessed moving objects and screaming, while the BBC sent a camera crew, but the disturbing footage they caught turned out to be unusable due to twisted recording components.

Below: Photographer Graham Morris (left) examines the evidence with Peggy Hodgson.

PARANORMAL ACTIVITY

Alone and still haunted, Peggy Hodgson contacted the Society of Psychical Research, an organization set up in 1882 to understand and explain events commonly known as psychic or paranormal, and were visited by two members, Maurice Grosse and Guy Lyon Playfair. Grosse was a British paranormal investigator and Playfair was a writer interested in parapsychology. Both men noticed that much of the activity was centered around Peggy's daughter, Janet. Playfair talked of "curious whistling and barking noises coming from Janet's general direction." Grosse spoke of toys being thrown seemingly unaided around the house, which, when picked up, were hot. "I was standing in the kitchen and a T-shirt leaped off the table and flew into the other side of the room while I was standing by it," he later said. Together they witnessed and photographed beds levitating, sofas moving, and children seemingly flung from their beds.

Below: An overturned settee was found in the Hodgsons' sitting room, but who—or what— overturned it?

On one occasion, Grosse and a neighbor were alarmed by one of the kids screaming, "I can't move! It's holding my leg!" Both would state that the child's leg was in the grip of an invisible hand. It seemed something was living in the house. Janet, who continued to be affected most by the haunting, talked of a feeling that whatever "evil" was in that house, it wanted to be "part of the family." She also spoke of an old man by the name of Bill Wilkins. Bill had apparently lived and died in the house years before. "It didn't want to hurt us. It had died there and wanted to be at rest. The only way it could communicate was through me and my sister." Recordings were made of Janet talking, but with a gruff old voice, supposed to be that of Wilkins. "Just before I died," the voice was recorded to say through young Janet, "I went blind, and then I had a hemorrhage and I fell asleep and I died in the chair in the corner downstairs."

Life went on, and while the hauntings continued, the visitations of a priest over a long period made the incidents less regular and less violent. The children were bullied at school and called freaks, or, in Johnny's case, "the ghost boy." Over the years, the case has been recognized as one of the world's most compelling examples of paranormal activity—for the Hodgsons, the effects were everlasting. While books were written and films were made about the goings on in that unassuming house in suburbia, for the Hodgsons it was very, very real. "Even my brother," Janet recalled years later, "until the day he left that place after Mum died, would say, 'There's still something there. You'd feel like you were being watched.'"

Below: The haunted family pose for a photograph: Janet (around whom much of the activity centered), Margaret, Billy, and Johnny Hodgson on February 17, 1978.

— ALTERNATIVE —
THEORIES

The Enfield Hauntings attracted worldwide attention, and the events have been scrutinized by experts in the paranormal. Shortly after the hauntings subsided, Guy Lyon Playfair, the writer specializing in such matters, wrote a book called *This House is Haunted*. In it, he, along with Maurice Grosse, concluded that while there were some doubts about some of the incidents, the hauntings were genuine. Others disagreed, pointing to Playfair's own admission of seeing Janet bend spoons with her hands while she thought she wasn't being watched, and using brooms to bang on ceilings, knowing people were upstairs. Skeptics alluded to the recordings made supposedly of the old man, Bill Wilkins, and claimed that they were produced by the girl's false vocal chords, which could create deep, guttural sounds. They also found that the vocabulary used was that of a child. An American ventriloquist stated that the voices were created by a vocal trick. What can't be explained is the moving furniture, witnessed by several

Above: Did Janet and her sister summon the mischievous spirits by playing with a Ouija board?

people, including the police officer who first arrived the night the hauntings started. Later, Janet admitted that 2 percent of the hauntings were her and her siblings trying to trick the investigators, but that she and her sister had played with a Ouija board just days before the hauntings began.

When the Hodgsons moved out, the Bennetts moved in. Two months later, having learned of the home's history, and after hearing voices and seeing an old man, they moved out.

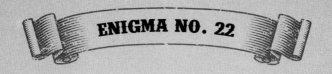

WAS MERCY BROWN A VAMPIRE?

Date: January 1892
Location: Exeter, Rhode Island

A village suffers an unexplained epidemic: one family is decimated, and the father is talked into exhuming the bodies of those he has lost. What he finds terrifies the community.

For centuries, a fear of the undead and vampires has gripped and entertained us. From Bram Stoker's dashing Count to teenage love stories, tales of pale-faced, bloodsucking villains and heroes have never been far from our consciousness.

By the first half of the eighteenth century, with an increase in communication and travel, reports started to appear in Western Europe. "The first mention of the word 'vampire' in the English language is in the 1730s," says author Roger Luckhurst, who edited the Oxford World's Classics reprint of *Dracula*, "in newspapers which carry reports from the edge of Europe, of bodies being dug up and looking bloated, and having fresh blood around their mouths."

VAMPIRES IN THE NEW WORLD

In the Northeast of America, settlers from Europe building new lives and communities were very much prone to a real fear of the undead.

In 1810 the body of Annie Dennett of rural New Hampshire was exhumed in the hope that her father, himself very sick, might be saved. All the villagers found was a couple of bones. In 1817 a family in Vermont, educated and "well respected," had their father's body exhumed, in the hope of saving sick relatives. His heart was burned in a blacksmith's forge.

And then there is the case of Mercy Brown—perhaps the most infamous vampire case in the Western world, and one that happened only eight years prior to the twentieth century. George and Mary Brown had set up home in Rhode Island with their children and lived a normal life in the town of Exeter. In the early 1880s, Mary fell ill and quickly died. In 1888 the eldest daughter, Mary Olive, also died, and then in January 1892 Mercy fell ill and she, too, passed away. Then just weeks later, George's son, Edwin, fell ill. Weak, pale, and thin, surely it wouldn't be long before he followed his poor relatives to the cemetery?

Above: In the hope of saving sick relatives, bodies were exhumed and hearts burned in blacksmiths' forges.

GRUESOME FINDINGS

It was then that George's fellow villagers got involved. Others had taken ill, but such was the ferocity with which this apparent epidemic had fallen upon the Brown family, the town's officials went to George and convinced him that the reason for the deaths in their village might well be one of his dead loved ones, and that the only way to be certain was to dig them all up. George agreed, desperate to save his son. When the coffins of his wife, Mary, and his daughter Mary Olive were opened, their bodies were normally decomposed. When Mercy's casket was opened, the body—two months after her death—was intact.

That winter, a hard frost had enveloped Rhode Island and, with frozen ground, they had been unable to bury Mercy's coffin. The casket had instead been stored above ground, and the cold air would surely account for a dead body with no signs of decay, but the locals were stunned to notice that her hair and nails had grown. She had also, it was said, moved from the position in which she was buried. On top of that, after an autopsy, they found liquid blood in her heart and liver.

Immediate fears of old superstition were given very real credence. Stories of sightings soon spread, with many stating they had seen Mercy walking at night. The legend of Mercy Brown, the Rhode Island vampire, had been born.

George, understandably upset by the gruesome discovery, was panicked enough to go to a physician, who, despite being a modern man of science, persuaded the grief-stricken father to allow him to remove Mercy's heart, burn it, and feed the ashes to his son, Edwin. This was an often-practiced ritual, but it didn't work. Edwin passed away.

Below: Eventually, Mercy Brown's heartless body was buried in Exeter's Baptist Church cemetery, and over a century later, curious tourists still seek out her tombstone.

— ALTERNATIVE —
THEORIES

Despite German scientist Robert Koch discovering the bacteria that causes TB in 1882, the vast majority of people had no idea of its contagious nature. By the time of Mercy's death, the illness was the leading cause of death across the country. The symptoms— weight loss, extreme fatigue, and a deathly color—would of course feed the fear of vampires, while diseases such as porphyria have long produced symptoms that have further fueled superstition. Centuries ago, porphyria was common in Eastern Europe, and as it affected hemoglobin levels in the blood, it produced severe skin rashes and meant that patients would suffer adverse effects to sunlight. It would also cause receding gums, so sufferers would have prominent-looking and sometimes even sharp-looking teeth. Early misunderstandings of the disease rabies have also been said to account for early fables about werewolves, as patients would display rabid, feral symptoms.

Above: In severe cases of porphyria, patients would lose their nose or ears, and so it isn't hard to see where the image of the famous and gruesome vampire Nosferatu stemmed from.

What remains unexplained is the fact that Mercy Brown was lying in a different position to that in which she was laid to rest. Perhaps it is best if we never know why...

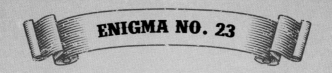

WHY DID IT RAIN ON THE RAIN MAN?

Date: 1983
Location: Stroudsburg, Pennsylvania

Donald Decker was a troubled young man, who, one week in 1983, became inexplicably surrounded by rain and mist. He would become known as the "Rain Man."

In late February 1983, 21-year-old Donnie Decker was granted a seven-day furlough from the 12-month prison sentence he had been handed for receiving stolen goods in New York. He was returning to Pennsylvania to attend the funeral of his grandfather, James Kishaugh. A well-behaved and placid prisoner, the prison services felt it only right that Decker should be allowed the time to both mourn and look after his bereaved family. Decker was pleased to get out of his cell, even for a matter of days, but what no one knew—not even his parents—was that he wouldn't be mourning the loss of his grandfather. Quite the opposite. Decker traveled home with a secret, and stood as family members shed tears, feeling nothing but pain, not for his grandfather's death but for what his grandfather had done to Decker in life.

Kishaugh had physically abused Decker. From the age of seven, the boy had been terrified of his grandfather, but unable to tell anyone; that fear had turned to hate. Decker went to the funeral, hoping that the nightmare could be buried with his grandfather.

"No other part of the family knew anything about what had happened, and it was like good fighting evil," he would later say. "The evil was gone, and I was hoping that everything would change." Decker would walk from the funeral in hope. That night, events suggested that things would indeed change—but not for the better. Staying with his friends Bob and Jeannie Keiffer, Decker excused himself from the dining table, complaining of feeling ill. His friends, thinking that the day must have taken its toll, suggested he go upstairs.

Below: Decker was hoping that the burial of his abusive grandfather would signal a fresh start; instead, it brought about a further series of terrifying events.

In the bathroom, Decker noticed the temperature drop. He would later describe the image of an old man—his grandfather, perhaps, but he couldn't be sure. Confused and scared, Decker then felt a scratching pain in his arm as three bloody marks appeared. Feeling faint and disoriented, he returned to the dining room. It was then that his friends saw that he was almost in a trance; they described their guest as not reacting to their words or physical touch. Decker would come in and out of these almost catatonic states… until it happened.

Below: From a few drops and a low mist to horizontal rain and cascading water, the Rain Man's symptoms were witnessed by several people.

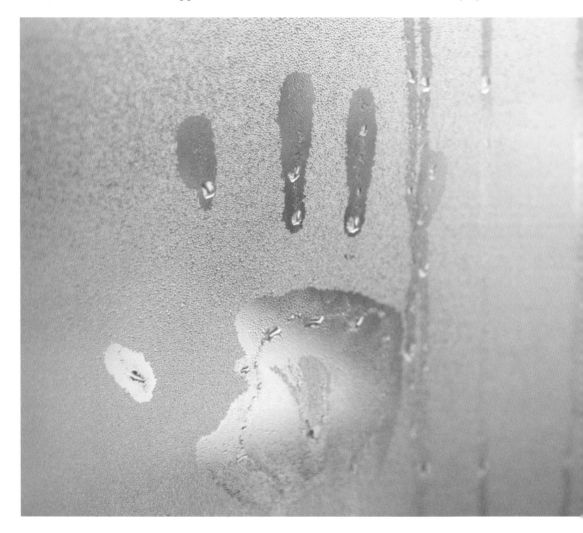

THE DEVIL'S RAIN

First a drip… rolling down the wall from the ceiling… followed by a low mist forming on the ground. The Keiffers were terrified and rang Rob Van Why, their landlord, hoping he could come by and explain what was happening. He couldn't. He pragmatically suggested a problem with the plumbing, but, "There were no pipes in the front end of the house to leak," Van Why later said. Perplexed, the landlord called his wife and the police. Patrolman Richard Wolbert was astonished by what he found. Water was falling from the ceiling like raindrops. Raindrops that defied any kind of logic. "I was met with this droplet of water traveling horizontally," Wolbert said. More police were called, but it was suggested that a clearly upset Decker and the Keiffers leave for a nearby restaurant. The police— the hairs on their arms standing up on end—were even more astounded to see that with Decker gone, the rain stopped.

The nearby restaurant was owned by Pam Scrofano, a friend of Van Why, and on hearing of the events and studying Decker, she tentatively suggested that it sounded like a possession. Upon learning of the funeral, Pam suggested the possession was being conducted by something evil. It was then that Decker's trance-like state returned and the water started again, but this time in the restaurant.

With water cascading down the walls and mist rising from the floor, Scrofano went to her office and picked up a crucifix, which she placed on Decker's skin, only to be alarmed by Decker's pain; it had burned him. The Keiffers took Decker back to their home, but with the water returning with them, and pots and pans moving and breaking in the kitchen,

Van Why angrily accused Decker of somehow damaging his property. It was then that the "possession" became more violent.

THE END OF A POSSESSION

Decker, seemingly levitating, was thrown backward, while an officer's crucifix once again burned his skin on contact. By now, the police chief had been called, but skeptical and keen to get his officers out, he declared that the incident was down to the plumbing, and that none of his men should investigate further. However, intrigued officers John Rundle and Bill Davies did return, finding Decker in even greater distress, claw marks visible on his neck and once again being violently thrown from his feet. A now very concerned Van Why called several priests but only one agreed to come, and Decker only found solace from his ordeal after extensive prayer.

With Decker's furlough over, he had to return to prison. In his cell, he realized that he could, if he concentrated, control the water. The guards didn't believe him, laughing and egging him on to make it rain in the warden's office. Decker obliged, and the warden, David Keenhold, was suddenly and without explanation drenched. Decker and Keenhold sat and talked about the ordeal, before the latter called a friend, the Reverend William Blackburn. At first Decker was angry; then, a terrible, a terrible, unearthly smell filled the cell, and the strange rain and mist began—or, as the reverend described it, "The Devil's rain."

Blackburn spent days sitting and praying with Decker. Clearly benefitting from the time spent with the reverend, Decker became more settled, until the rain stopped. "I think what happened was my grandfather's doing," Decker later said. "Because he abused me when I was young, he got a chance to abuse me again."

ALTERNATIVE
THEORIES

Left: At first burned by the cross, but later saved by it—was the Rain Man possessed by a demonic infestation of his grandfather?

There are many skeptics who think that the case of Don Decker, the Rain Man, is an elaborate hoax, concocted by several people who were unable to produce any photographic evidence, despite the events happening over a number of days. However, all these people came from very different places and backgrounds—police officers, restaurant owners, priests, prison guards, and wardens. None sought financial gain. Two paranormal researchers, Chip Decker (no relation) and Peter Jordan, studied the case and Jordan, while not completely convinced, was intrigued by the events: "The Donald Decker case is by far the singularly most fascinating and important case I have ever personally been involved with," he said. "That does not mean I believe that it necessarily is proof positive to me of demonic infestation. But it is the case, in my own personal experience, up to this point, that comes the closest to that hypothesis."

ENIGMATIC CREATURES

There are an estimated 8.7 million species of animals in the world today, but scientists have said that the vast majority of them have yet to be identified, so they remain a mystery. This chapter explores some of the peculiar animals that have only been fleetingly sighted and are still waiting to be properly identified. Are these strange and sometimes terrifying creatures real, or just figments of over-active imaginations? No one is quite sure.

Take, for instance, the Jersey Devil, a cross between a kangaroo and a dragon, with hooves and a forked tail, which was said to have terrorized the US state that gave it its name in the early 1900s. The Mothman was described as a cross between a man and a bird, with bright red eyes. Standing at 7 feet (2 meters) high, for 13 months in 1966 and 1967, it could be seen flying in the skies above a small town in West Virginia. The Chupacabra is another creature that has struck fear into all those who have crossed its path. First sighted in Puerto Rico in 1995, it earned its name for allegedly killing animals and then draining them of their blood. The beast of Bodmin Moor in England was reported to be a large cat that would prowl this area of Cornwall and slaughter livestock. There have been reports of this beast since 1983, but, like all of these animals, it remains a mystery as to whether it actually exists.

Left: Real or faked? True stories or folklore? For the Chupacabra, the legend, at least, is very much alive.

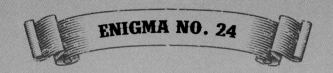

WAS THE JERSEY DEVIL THE RESULT OF A CURSE, OR OF MASS HYSTERIA?

Date: 1735–Present day
Location: New Jersey

A strange devil-like creature has been said to inhabit a forest near the coast of New Jersey for nearly three centuries now.

In the early eighteenth century Deborah Leeds lived with her husband and their 12 children in Pine Barrens, a dense forest on the coastal plain of southern New Jersey. When she discovered she was pregnant for the thirteenth time, Leeds was not at all happy, and in her fury cursed the child and declared that it would be the Devil. When the child was born, Mother Leeds is believed to have yelled, "Oh, let this one be a devil!" Accounts differ as to whether the child emerged as a creature, or became one as soon as it was born, but it began to scream, killed the attending midwife, and disappeared through the chimney to haunt the surrounding area. The creature would become known in folklore as the "Jersey Devil" and has been described as a cross between a kangaroo and a dragon.

IT'S ALL IN THE NAME

There were very few early sightings of the devil, and the legend was fueled more by a local politician of the time named Daniel Leeds, almost entirely because he shared a name with the family who had produced the devil. To begin with, the creature was better known as the "Leeds Devil." Daniel Leeds was a young Quaker who arrived in America in the late 1600s and settled in New Jersey, before becoming involved in local politics and embarking on the writing of an almanac. He was also a royal surveyor and a staunch supporter of America remaining part of the British Empire, which made him unpopular. Leeds also earned disapproval for publishing stories about astrology, angels, magic, and Christian occultism, which were dismissed as pagan by many at the time. Furious locals would call him a monster or a devil.

Leeds' son Titan inherited the family business from his father, who died in 1720, and continued to publish the almanac, which would feature a dragon-like creature on the cover; he would find himself in competition with Benjamin Franklin, who published a rival almanac. Franklin predicted Leeds' death, and when it happened, he would speak about him as a ghostly and devil-like presence. By the middle of the nineteenth century, Titan Leeds being cast as a devil kept the legend alive.

Below: Daniel Leeds was discredited on account of his occult and pagan stories, and his son kept the Leeds Devil legend alive.

SIGHTINGS AND HYSTERIA

The first report of the Leeds Devil was in October 1887, in the *Elkhart Sentinel*. "Whenever he went near it, it would give a most unearthly yell that frightened the dogs. 'That thing,' said the colonel, 'is not a bird nor an animal, but it is the Leeds Devil, according to the description, and it was born over in Evesham, Burlington county, a hundred years ago … There isn't a family in Burlington or any of the adjoining counties that does not know of the Leeds Devil, and it was the bugaboo to frighten children with when I was a boy.'"

There were further reported sightings in Bridgeton in 1873, and tracks in the snow at Haddonfield, Leeds Point, and Brigantine in 1894. Then, during a week in January 1909, hundreds of people claimed to have seen the Jersey Devil and newspapers were full of reports, as a mood of mass hysteria consumed the area.

Thack Cozzens claimed to have seen the creature as he was leaving a hotel in Woodbury: "I heard a hissing and something white flew across the street. I saw two spots of phosphorus, the eyes of the beast. There was a white cloud, like escaping steam from an engine. It moved as fast as an auto." The creature was next seen by a policeman in Bristol, Pennsylvania, and was believed to have killed a puppy in the town of Riverside, New Jersey.

Above: The Jersey Devil is reported to stand on two hooved feet, and has a long neck with the head of a goat or horse, short arms with claws, large bat-like wings, and a forked tail.

On January 20, the creature was seen in Trenton, before midnight, by William Cromley, who saw it standing in the road, before it hissed, spread its wings, and flew away. It soon arrived at the house of Claudius P. Weeden, who heard wings flapping and saw its hoofprints in the snow.

Philadelphia Zoo supposedly offered $10,000 to anyone who could capture the creature, or provide a sample of its feces, so they could better understand what it was. Since the hysteria of 1909, the sightings have slowed but there were some in the 1930s, 1950s, 1960s, and as recently as 2015, when Dave Black claimed to have seen the Devil in the woods at Little Egg Harbor, New Jersey.

— ALTERNATIVE —
THEORIES

Even though the Jersey Devil was said to have been born over 280 years ago, there have been almost no credible sightings of it, and it is hard to argue with those who suggest it is just an urban myth and a piece of local folklore. "There are no photographs, no bones, no hard evidence whatsoever, and worst of all, no explanation of its origins that doesn't require belief in the supernatural," Jeff Brunner of the Humane Society of New Jersey has said. His theory is that any sightings of the creature have in fact been of the sandhill crane, an unusually large bird with a sizeable wingspan.

The glut of sightings in 1909 has been attributed to mass hysteria, with people whipping each other up without having seen anything. During the hysteria, a showman in Philadelphia announced that the Devil was actually an Australian vampire, before declaring he had captured it and had it on display at his 9th and Arch Street Museum. The "vampire" was, in fact, a kangaroo painted green, with wings glued to its back, and which was placed in a poorly lit cage, where a boy at the back would poke it.

Below: Showman Jacob Hope later admitted that his kangaroo "vampire" was a hoax.

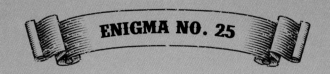

ENIGMA NO. 25

HAVE YOU SEEN THE BIG GRAY MAN OF BEN MACDHUI?

Date: Since 1891
Location: The Cairngorms, Scotland

At the top of a Scottish mountain lurks a towering figure that has scared walkers for more than a century.

At nearly 4,300 feet (1,300 meters) Ben MacDhui is the second highest mountain in the United Kingdom and a part of the Cairngorms mountain range. Its summit is shrouded in mist and snow, and hikers who reach the top often feel a huge sense of achievement; but for over a century they have also on occasion felt something altogether more sinister: the presence of a mysterious towering figure known in folklore as the Big Gray Man of Ben MacDhui. Also known in Gaelic as *Am Fear Liath Mòr*, or more simply as Grayman, he has been described as a dark, thin, 10-foot (3-meter) creature covered in short brown hair, who stalks climbers who reach the summit of his mountain. There have been some sightings, but climbers have mostly spoken about hearing Grayman walking behind them in the mist, his footsteps crunching on the gravel.

The first account of the Big Gray Man was provided by Professor J. Norman Collie of University College London, who was a fellow of the Royal Geographical Society and a past president of the Alpine Club. In 1925 he told the Cairngorm club about his experience at the summit of Ben MacDhui many years earlier, in 1891: "I was returning from the cairn on the summit in a mist when I began to think I heard something else than merely the noise of my own footsteps," Collie told them. "Every few steps I took,

Above: The ascent path up Ben MacDhui is rocky and gravelly, allowing any footsteps to be heard easily.

Above: Experienced hiker Professor J. Norman Collie gave the first account of a possible encounter with Grayman—and swore never to return to the mountain.

I heard a crunch and then another crunch, as if someone was walking after me but taking steps three or four times the length of my own. I said to myself, this is all nonsense. I listened and heard it again but could see nothing in the mist. As I walked on and the eerie crunch, crunch sounded behind me, I was seized with terror and took to my heels, staggering blindly among the boulders for four or five miles nearly down to Rothiemurchus Forest. Whatever you make of it, I do not know, but there is something very queer about the top of Ben MacDhui and I will not go back there again."

FOOTSTEPS IN THE MIST

In 1904 the climber Hugh D. Welsh was camping at the same summit with his brother, when during both the day and the night they could hear a noise they described as like "slurring footsteps, as if someone was walking through water-saturated gravel." Welsh added that he and his brother were "frequently conscious of something near us, an eerie sense of apprehension," and so on his return to Derry Lodge he reported this to the head stalker, who replied, "That would have been the *Fear Liath Mòr* you heard."

In May 1945 Peter Densham, who carried out rescue work in the Cairngorms during World War II, reported the mist closing in and hearing a series of strange noises. He recalled that he felt someone was near to him, with pressure being applied to his neck, and crunching footsteps around him. He admitted running away before he saw anything.

THE SWAGGERING GIANT

Another climber, Richard Frere, who had worked with Densham during the war on the mountain, spoke about the experience of a friend of his, whom he did not name, who spent a night camping on Ben MacDhui as a test of his nerve and to win a bet. On his own, Frere's friend found himself becoming scared and uncomfortable, and recalled that, "it was as if he was an unwilling recipient of new revolutionary thought impulses built up in some all-powerful mind." After he had fallen asleep in his tent, he soon woke with a sense of dread and could see a large figure standing outside the tent in front of the moon, until it walked away. He peered out from the tent, and "about 20 yards away, a great brown creature was swaggering down the hill." Frere's friend described the creature as being around 20 feet (6 meters) tall and, crucially, with "an air of insolent strength about it."

Below: Swirling mists, the sound of footsteps, and large, looming figures are the trademarks of a Big Gray sighting.

In 1958 the mountaineer Alexander Tewnion wrote in *The Scots Magazine* about his own encounter with the Big Gray Man, which had occurred back in October 1943. "I spent a 10-day leave climbing alone in the Cairngorms. One afternoon, just as I reached the summit cairn of Ben MacDhui, mist swirled across the Lairig Ghru and enveloped the mountain. The atmosphere became dark and oppressive, a fierce, bitter wind whisked among the boulders, and ... an odd sound echoed through the mist—a loud footstep, it seemed. Then another, and another ... A strange shape loomed up, receded, came charging at me! Without hesitation I whipped out the revolver and fired three times at the figure. When it still came on I turned and hared down the path, reaching Glen Derry in a time that I have never bettered. You may ask was it really the *Fear Liath Mòr*? Frankly, I think it was."

There have been no photographs and no hard evidence of the existence of the Big Gray Man of Ben MacDhui, only the terrified sightings of solitary hikers at the summit. The photographer John A. Rennie had thought he had found Grayman's footprints in the snow, 19 inches (48 cm) long and 14 inches (36 cm) wide, in the Spey Valley, about 15 miles (25 kilometers) from the mountain. He published the photographs in his book *Romantic Strathspey*, only years later to see these footprints form in the snow in front of his very eyes as it rained, and was forced to admit his mistake and that they had nothing to do with any creature.

Below: The mist that typically rolls across the tops of the Cairngorms could play a key role in the apparitions.

— ALTERNATIVE —
THEORIES

In 1791 the poet James Hogg was on Ben MacDhui and reported seeing "a giant blackamoor, at least 30 feet high, and equally proportioned, and very near me. I was actually struck powerless with astonishment and terror." He fled in panic, but the next day returned and thought he could see this creature again, until he took off his hat and saw the creature was doing the same, forcing him to realize it had been his shadow in the fog all along.

Above: Does the phenomenon of Brocken specters explain what hikers really saw on Ben MacDhui?

More than two centuries later, the leading explanation for the Big Gray Man is that he has always been an optical illusion, imagined by exhausted and isolated hikers. Such an optical illusion at the top of a mountain has a specific name: "Brocken specters," first discovered by Johann Silberschlag, from the Prussian Academy of Sciences, in 1780 at the top of the Brocken, the highest peak in northern Germany. There, Silberschlag realized that in foggy and wet conditions, with the sun penetrating from a low angle, he could see his own shadow in the fog. The subject's shadow is invariably a lot larger than the subject, producing the illusion of a tall, intimidating figure…

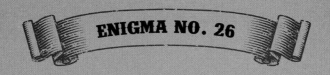

WHY DO DOGS JUMP OFF OVERTOUN BRIDGE?

Date: Since the 1950s
Location: Overtoun House, Scotland

There is a bridge in Scotland reputed to be surrounded by ghosts and dark spirits, where a succession of dogs have thrown themselves to their deaths.

In the grounds of historic Overtoun House in West Dunbartonshire, Scotland, Overtoun Bridge spans a stream and waterfall. It is a grand arched structure, which, since the 1950s, has become known as the site where an estimated 600 dogs have thrown themselves off the bridge, and as many as 50 have died after falling 50 feet (15 meters).

In 2004 Kenneth Meikle was walking across the bridge with his family, when his dog, a Golden Retriever called Hendrix, bolted and leaped off the bridge. "My daughter screamed, and I ran down the bank to where the dog lay and carried her up to safety," Meikle said. "As I did so, her hair started to fall out. It must have been shock because when we got her home, she shook all night." In 2005, when five dogs in the space of six months had jumped to their deaths, Donna Cooper was walking in the grounds of Overtoun House with her husband, son, and their Collie. As soon as they began to cross the bridge, the dog suddenly leaped over a parapet and fell to his death. In 2014 Alice Trevorrow was walking her three-year-old Springer Spaniel Cassie near the bridge. "I had parked up and as she is so obedient I didn't put her lead on," she recalled. "Me and my son walked toward Cassie, who was staring at something above the bridge … she definitely saw something that made her jump. There is something sinister going on. It was so out of character for her."

CAN DOGS COMMIT SUICIDE?

It has become known as the "Dog Suicide Bridge," but are these pets choosing to end their life? Some experts have argued dogs can absorb emotions from their owners. If owners are depressed, they can transfer it to their dog; but, when interviewed, the owners of the dogs did not admit to harboring suicidal thoughts.

Below: Why have so many dogs felt compelled to throw themselves off the bridge? Are the dogs committing suicide? What is luring them to take such a potentially dangerous leap?

Most experts are highly dismissive of the idea these dogs could intentionally kill themselves. The dog behaviorist Stan Rawlinson has said, "A dog can get depressed, certainly, and it can get anxious. But what it couldn't do is commit suicide, because that would need a decision on a moralistic basis, and dogs, unlike humans, do not have the same moral sense." Kendal Sheppard, a veterinarian behavioral specialist, stated: "Human suicide is usually precipitated by a feeling that tomorrow will not be any better than today. But there is no evidence to suggest dogs have a sense of now and tomorrow."

There has been a pattern to the events surrounding most of the dog jumping; it has always been at the same spot by the final two parapets, on a clear sunny day, and the dogs of a breed with a long snout, and so possessing an exceptionally strong sense of smell. The canine psychologist Dr. David Sands has argued that the dogs have been lured by the smell of urine from minks nestled beneath the bridge. The mink's powerful anal glands produce a strong, musty odor that grips dogs and makes them want to approach immediately. The leaps have occurred on dry, sunny days when this smell would have been at its strongest. In addition, these strange leaps began in the 1950s, when mink began to breed in large numbers in Scotland.

Below: There are around 26,000 mink in Scotland—including those nestling under the Overtoun Bridge.

"When you get down to a dog's level, the solid granite of the bridge's walls obscures their vision and blocks out all sound," Dr. Sands said. "The one sense not obscured, smell, goes into overdrive. I think it was highly likely at Overtoun Bridge that it was curiosity that killed the dog."

ALTERNATIVE
THEORIES

Glaswegian teacher Paul Owens contends that Overtoun House has witnessed a glut of supernatural activity over the years and has called it a "thin place," where Earth and Heaven are close. The bridge is a site where ghosts come to visit the living world. Author of *The Baron of Rainbow Bridge: Overtoun's Death Leaping Dogs Mystery Unraveled*, Owens has argued that dogs are sensitive to the supernatural world, and the presence of ghosts has caused them to leap from the bridge. "When Baron Overtoun, who built the bridge, died in 1908, she [Lady Overtoun] was said to have wandered the bridge, grief stricken, for years," Owens said. "It is thought by some to be her presence that lingers here."

In recent years a photograph has been produced showing the ghost of Lady Overtoun looking out over the estate from an upstairs window in Overtoun House. Fueling the belief that dark spirits hover over the bridge, in October

Above: Rather than mink, is it dark spirits that lure dogs to their death?

1994, Kevin Moy threw his two-week-old son Eoghan to his death from there, as he believed he was the Devil. Moy, who was suffering from depression, believed his son's birthmark had been put there by the Devil himself, and that he would destroy the world by infecting mankind with a virus. He was found not guilty of murder as he was declared insane, and was detained in a mental health hospital.

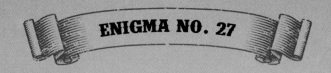

ENIGMA NO. 27

WAS THE MOTHMAN AN OMEN OR A PRANK?

Date: November 1966–December 1967
Location: Point Pleasant, West Virginia

A creature described as a terrifying cross between a man and a bird—the "Mothman"—was seen flying around a small town in West Virginia for more than a year before disaster struck.

On the evening of November 12, 1966, Kenneth Duncan and four other men were digging a grave for his brother-in-law in Clendenin, West Virginia, when what he called "a brown human being" flew over their heads. "It was gliding through the trees and was in sight for about a minute," Duncan explained. He went on to describe it as being a bird-like figure with large, bright red eyes that glowed in the night sky, and a wingspan of around 10 feet (3 meters).

Three days later, two couples reported seeing this man–bird creature hovering in the sky above them in the TNT area of the town (named after a World War II munitions site). "It was like a man with wings," Steve Mallette told the *Point Pleasant Register*. "It wasn't like anything you'd see on TV or in a monster movie…

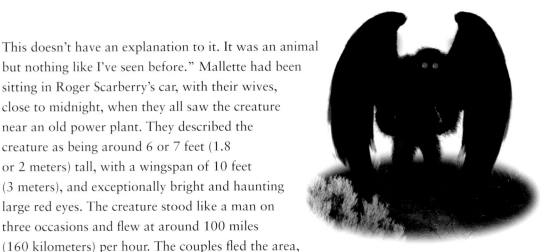

This doesn't have an explanation to it. It was an animal but nothing like I've seen before." Mallette had been sitting in Roger Scarberry's car, with their wives, close to midnight, when they all saw the creature near an old power plant. They described the creature as being around 6 or 7 feet (1.8 or 2 meters) tall, with a wingspan of 10 feet (3 meters), and exceptionally bright and haunting large red eyes. The creature stood like a man on three occasions and flew at around 100 miles (160 kilometers) per hour. The couples fled the area, but the creature then followed them around Point Pleasant, hovering above their car. "We went downtown, turned around and went back, and there it was again," Mallette said. "It seemed to be waiting on us." The police went to the scene two hours after the couples had claimed to have seen the creature but were unable to find it.

On the same night, Newell Partridge, who lived 100 miles (160 kilometers) to the north of Point Pleasant, believed the same creature was responsible for the disappearance of his German Shepherd, Bandit. Partridge first saw the creature in a field next to his house in Doddridge County and shone a flashlight on it, revealing its huge red eyes reflecting back at him. His dog went to investigate in the field, and never returned. And three days later, two Point Pleasant volunteer firemen in the TNT area where the couples had come across the creature saw what they described as a "large bird with red eyes."

Above: The Mothman was described as being taller than a man, with a large wingspan, and glowing red eyes.

EMBRACING THE LEGEND

This creature would become known as "the Mothman," a mythical flying figure that appeared to be cross between a man and a large bird, which was regularly sighted around the Point Pleasant area between November 1966 and December 1967. The small West Virginian town has come to embrace the legend, and since 2002 has staged the Mothman Festival every September, which draws around 2,000 people, many of whom travel to the TNT area to try and see the Mothman for themselves. There is also a Mothman museum, which opened in 2005, and a 12-foot (3.6-meter) metallic statue of the Mothman, which has stood proudly in the town since 2003. The Mothman has become a tourist attraction—you can buy a Mothman pizza or Mothman frappuccino on your visit—but its presence in the 1960s was also seen as a bad omen, and came to be seen as the signal for an imminent disaster.

On December 15, 1967, the Silver Bridge, which spanned the Ohio River and connected Point Pleasant with Gallipolis, Ohio, suddenly collapsed, killing 46 people. The bridge collapsed at rush hour, full of traffic, as people returned home from work and families went into town to do some Christmas shopping. The cause of the collapse was a defective eye-bar link that cracked and brought the whole bridge down, but the Mothman was believed to have played a role. Some witnesses to the collapse say they saw the Mothman right by the bridge just before the disaster. After the bridge's collapse, Mothman was almost never seen again in the town, which caused some to speculate that he had been there over the previous year to warn the residents of Point Pleasant about the impending disaster, while others suggested he had brought the disaster with him.

Below: Boats and cranes grimly drag the water after the rush-hour collapse of the Silver Bridge.

— ALTERNATIVE —
THEORIES

The TNT area, where the Mothman was first spotted, is surrounded by the McClintic Wildlife Management Area—a bird sanctuary, full of owls. All those who claimed to have seen the creature spoke about it having bright red eyes, which would reflect when exposed to light, and, as ornithologists have confirmed, many birds' eyes become bright red when caught by a flashlight or the headlights of a car. It has been speculated that the Mothman was actually a barn owl, a great horned owl (right), a barred owl, or a snowy owl.

During the Mothman hysteria, Point Pleasant resident Asa Henry shot and killed a snowy owl, which is today stuffed, mounted, and displayed in the town. Mr. Henry's grandson, David Pyles, recalled that his grandfather, who never believed in the Mothman, always pointed out that once he had killed this owl, there were virtually no more sightings.

Above: There is a real possibility that people were mistaking large owls for the Mothman.

In the week the Mothman was first seen, Dr. Robert L. Smith, an associate professor of wildlife biology at the University of West Virginia, had stated his belief that the creature was probably a sandhill crane, the second biggest crane in the US. This bird can often appear to be as tall as a man and has a wingspan of around 7 feet (3 meters). Reports of bright red eyes could be explained by the red circles of flesh around a sandhill's eyes.

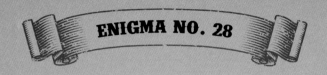

IS THERE A BEAST ROAMING BODMIN MOOR?

Date: Since 1983
Location: Cornwall, England

A large wild cat is said to roam Bodmin Moor, scaring the locals and slaughtering their livestock—but to this day, it has never been caught.

Since 1983 there have been more than 60 sightings of an unusually large wild cat, possibly a panther or a puma, roaming Bodmin Moor in southwest England. Local farmers have said this creature is either black or brown, with a long tail, and has stalked the moor for many years. After a spate of sightings in the 1990s, one farmer, John Goodenough, claimed he had lost up to £1,000 worth of livestock to attacks from the wild cat: "You'll know when the Beast's there. There'll be no rabbits or foxes about and the birds stop singing. That's the call for caution. And the way they kill. If it's a dog, there's wool and trouble everywhere. A cat goes in, kills and eats. There is very little mess."

In August 1994 the Member of Parliament for Cornwall North, Paul Tyler, reacted to the concerns of these farmers and convened a conference to urgently address the matter. In January 1995 the

Ministry of Agriculture, Fisheries and Food (MAFF) thought the sightings and concerns serious enough to commission an investigation. Mammal biologist Simon Baker and zoologist Charlie Wilson headed up the investigation, and looked at the available evidence, which included speaking to those who claimed to have seen the wild cat, an examination of sheep carcasses killed by it, and the tracks left by it. They also looked at photographic and video evidence, and visited the locations where this footage had been taken to ascertain the scale of the animal.

Above: Mrs. Rhodes from Ninestones Farm said the beast killed 10 of her sheep, and that she had seen it herself: "Its eyes are great yellow orbs. And it has a foul scream like a woman's, but 100 times magnified."

NO VERIFIABLE EVIDENCE

In July 1995 the report concluded that, "No verifiable evidence for the presence of a 'big cat' was found … There is no significant threat to livestock from a 'big cat' on Bodmin Moor." Baker and Wilson had found that the carcasses did not show any signs of being mauled by big cats and that the tracks were made by large dogs. The photographic evidence, they believed, was nothing more than domestic cats. If there were any exotic cats present on Bodmin Moor, Wilson believed they were probably descendants of cats released because of the 1976 Dangerous Wild Animals Act.

Many locals believed the findings to be either a government cover-up or a shoddy investigation that didn't look into the matter deeply enough. Paul Tyler MP wrote in the *Daily Telegraph*, "The mystery has not been solved, but deepened. Farmers and others who had sighted the so-called 'Beast of Bodmin Moor' did not take kindly to being portrayed as gullible yokels."

CAPTURING NEW EVIDENCE

A week after the government had issued their disputed findings, a 14-year-old boy was walking along the River Fowey when he stumbled across the skull of an unusually large cat. Could this be the remains of the beast? While its lower jaw was missing, there were still two long, sharp teeth. The skull was studied by the Natural History Museum in London, which confirmed that it was a genuine skull from a leopard, but that the animal had not died in Britain. It had been killed elsewhere and brought to Bodmin. There were also the remains of an eggshell inside the skull from a cockroach not found in Northern Europe.

In 1998 the beast was captured in a 20-second film, which showed a three-and-a-half-foot (one-meter) black cat. The Newquay Zoo curator and wild cat expert Mike Thomas declared the video "the best evidence yet" that there were large cats on Bodmin. After that, there was only the occasional sighting, until 2014, when 19-year-old student Henry Warren spotted what appeared to be the beast in a field near Bodmin Moor. "I was taking pictures of our new house when I saw something run across the field and in front of my lens. It was massive and was hopping up and down like a large cat; there's no way it was a fox or a dog." Despite continued sightings of the beast, definitive proof of the creature that roams Bodmin Moor has remained elusive.

Below: The skull thought to perhaps have been the beast's could have been imported as part of a leopardskin rug, because the skin had been cleanly cut and not ripped away or left to rot.

— ALTERNATIVE —
THEORIES

It has been speculated that three pumas were released into the wild around Dartmoor by the circus owner Mary Chipperfield after her zoo in Plymouth closed in 1978. While the cats were being taken to their new home, Chipperfield decided to release three of them into the wild—a breeding pair and another male. Danny Bumping of the British Big Cats Society told the *Daily Telegraph* in 2016 about how these pumas had come to be seen on Bodmin Moor: "In the 1970s Plymouth Zoo was owned by the Chipperfields, the circus family. When the zoo was shut down, Mary Chipperfield agreed to transfer her five pumas to Mr. Daw at Dartmoor Wildlife Park. When they arrived, Ellis [Daw] told me there were only two pumas in the consignment but five tags in the cage. Mary Chipperfield told Ellis she had broken down on Dartmoor and that somehow three of the pumas had escaped. We think she let them out on the moor." Mary Chipperfield died in

Above: Could pumas released onto the moor have survived in the English climate and with such a limited food supply?

2014, but her husband, Roger Cawley, dismissed the story as false, and said no pumas had ever been released by his late wife.

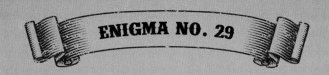
IS THE CHUPACABRA A DOG OR A FIGMENT OF THE IMAGINATION?

Date: 1995–Present day
Location: Worldwide

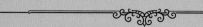

A strange creature that was said to kill animals and drain them of their blood was first sighted in Puerto Rico and then all around the world—but it has never been caught.

On an afternoon in August 1995, Madelyne Tolentino was helping her mother move into a new house in the Barrio Campo Rico neighborhood of Canóvanas in northeastern Puerto Rico. When she glanced out of the window she saw a man driving a car, who had a terrified look on his face—then she noticed that he was staring directly at a creature she describes as walking on two legs. From her vantage point, Tolentino was able to observe the creature, and described it in great detail: it had dark gray eyes that spread across its face to its temples; two little holes for a nose; and a slash for a mouth that it kept closed. It was around 4 feet (1 meter) tall, with long arms, which were constantly in the "attack position," and long skinny legs, with three toes on each foot. On its lower back was a collection of feathers or spikes.

"I even got down on the floor to see if it had genitals," Tolentino recalled. "It had nothing at all, it was 'plain' and 'sealed.' I was laughing and saying to my mother: 'What the heck is this? Does it defecate through its mouth after it eats?' It made robot-like movements, as if being controlled by someone." When Tolentino then saw the look in the creature's eyes, she screamed: "My God! Had that thing appeared in front of me I'd have broken into a run, but since I was behind the glass, and there was a gate outside the glass, I said to myself: 'That thing can't harm me in here.' Meanwhile, when my mother heard me scream, she decided to go out and get the creature … The thing took off running; I'm not sure if it was because I screamed or not."

Above: No real-life images exist but images have been created for film and media, going viral and fueling the intrigue of the creature. Puerto Ricans depict a chupacabra as bipedal, with a row of spikes running down its back, and skinny arms and legs.

Tolentino explained it began hopping like a kangaroo and fled to the woods opposite her mother's house. A boy who worked with her husband Miguel ran after it. When this boy caught up with the creature, it stood up and showed what he described as its feathers. It also opened its mouth and bared a set of large fangs before disappearing farther into the woods at such a speed the boy could not catch it. Later that day, other neighbors in Barrio Campo Rico reported that they had seen the same creature, with eyes that could light up the darkness.

BLOOD-SUCKING ANIMAL-KILLER

This was the first ever reported sighting of a creature that would become known as "Chupacabra," Spanish for "goat-sucker" (*chupar* is "to suck" and *cabra* is "goat"), as it was blamed for the deaths of hundreds of livestock, including goats, by draining them of their blood. It has been suggested that the Chupacabra was behind the death of up to 150 animals in the Canóvanas region during August 1995, and more than 2,000 animal mutilations that occurred throughout Puerto Rico in the seven months after that first sighting.

Below: Reported to have slaughtered hundreds of livestock, the Chupacabra also stands accused of ripping apart a teddy bear.

The mayor of Canóvanas, José Soto, led a group of volunteers armed with guns and a goat in a cage to find the Chupacabra, but they never got close to it. The Chupacabra was reported to have struck again in November 1995 in Puerto Rico, when a farmer found that dozens of his goats, cats, dogs, horses, turkeys, and rabbits had been killed, and all of their bodies drained of blood. Soon after, a resident on the island described seeing a creature with red eyes and hairy arms break into a house and rip apart a teddy bear.

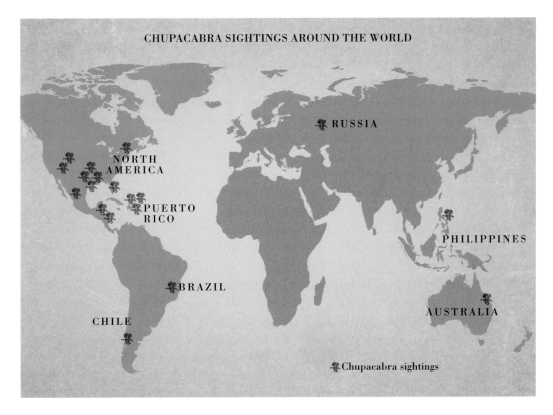

CHUPACABRA SIGHTINGS AROUND THE WORLD

In March 1996 the Chupacabra made it to the USA for the first time, sighted in a rural community outside of Miami, Florida, where it killed 40 animals. Two months later, in the Rio Grande Valley, Texas, a goat was killed, the Chupacabra leaving its trademark puncture wounds on it. It wasn't long before sightings were made farther afield than the Americas, but it was in Chile that the creature really made its mark.

Above: Other creatures fitting the description of the Chupacabra have been spotted mostly in the Americas, from Maine to Chile, but also as far away as Russia, the Philippines, and Australia.

TRAVELS TO CHILE

In 2000 a series of attacks in Calama, a rural farming community in Chile, managed to whip up an atmosphere of hysteria. Livestock was being killed with a single puncture to the throat, but no one could find the perpetrator. The National Guard in Chile were brought in, but around 100 armed soldiers found nothing on their search missions. The Ministry of Justice in the capital

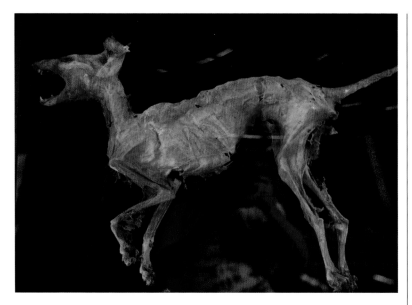

Left: A supposed chupacabra is safely housed in a showcase in Calico Ghost Town, California.

Below: This illustration by Alvin Padayachee depicts a Texan chupacabra as a hairless, doglike monster.

Santiago demanded answers and launched an investigation, which once again failed to find the Chupacabra, or any real evidence it even existed. The Chilean government issued a statement that blamed the attacks on a pack of wild dogs.

There was a flurry of sightings throughout the Americas until around 2000, when it suddenly became quiet, although reports of this creature being seen in the southern states of the USA continue to this day. The description was now different: it was thought to be a coyote or wild dog—probably with mange, as it was sometimes seen hairless—with an arched back, fangs, and claws.

— ALTERNATIVE —
THEORIES

Could the release of the Hollywood alien horror movie *Species* have influenced all the first sightings of the Chupacabra in the Americas in 1995? Loren Coleman, director of the International Cryptozoology Museum, certainly believes so: "If you look at the date when the movie *Species* opened in Puerto Rico, you will see that it overlaps with the first explosion of reports there," he said. "Then compare the images of Natasha Henstridge's creature character Sil and you will see the unmistakable spikes out the back that match those of the first images of the Chupacabra in 1995." The first ever witness in Puerto Rico, Madelyne Tolentino, admitted she had seen the movie a few weeks before her sighting. Tolentino could have seen a rhesus monkey, which can stand on its hind legs, and there was a group of them being used in blood experiments in Puerto Rico at the time. They could have possibly got loose, which would explain the multiple sightings of a strange creature.

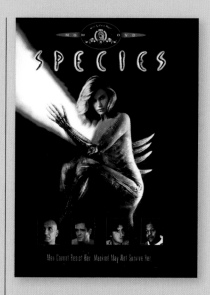

Above: With coinciding sighting/release dates, matching spinal spikes, and both being seen by the first ever witness, the Chupacabra and Sil had a lot in common.

Some have suggested that the US government was conducting a genetic experiment in the rainforests of Puerto Rico and accidentally created this animal. It is a theory that also took hold in Chile after its rash of sightings.

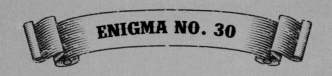

WAS THE ALTAMAHA-HA MONSTER CAUGHT ON FILM?

Date: March 2018
Location: Altamaha River, Georgia

In 2018 a man filmed the washed-up carcass of what he believed might be the underwater Altamaha-ha monster. Was it, or had he been hoaxed?

On the shores of the Altamaha River, in the southern state of Georgia, there lives, according to locals, an underwater animal—unidentified by science, but if those who have seen it are to be believed, resembling some sort of prehistoric beast.

In 1971 former newspaper publisher Larry Gwin was fishing with a friend when they both spotted a 30-foot (10-meter) long "animal with flippers like a seal." They said: "It had two big humps, about 5 feet apart, and left behind a wake like that of a speedboat." The story made the news, and more locals residing near the riverbanks came forward with stories of a large creature. One witness, Harry Blackman, claimed that what he saw (in the 1970s) had "a snake-like head, and was between 15 and 20 feet long." It seemed that the legendary Altamaha-ha monster, for so long talked about in the area, might just be real.

Tradition has it that before settlers arrived in the area, Native Americans who lived and hunted along the banks of the river spoke of a giant, snake-like animal that was often spotted, and in April 1830 the *Savannah Georgian* newspaper published a story about a Captain Delano, of a schooner called the *Eagle,* seeing something off St. Simons Island, at the mouth of the Altamaha. The report, verified by five other witnesses, read: "He repeated the ... particulars precisely, describing the animal he saw as being about 70 feet long, and its circumference about that of a sugar hogshead, moving with its head (shaped like an alligator's) about 8 feet out of the water."

Above: Jeff Warren and his son were on a fishing trip when they spied something prehistoric-looking on the shore.

CAUGHT ON CAMERA

In March 2018, Jeff Warren was taking a boat trip with his son when he spotted something lying on the shores of Georgia's Wolf Island National Wildlife Refuge. Since it looked like the remains of some sort of animal, he went to take a closer look. Once there, he was still none the wiser. From afar, Warren presumed the form was a dead or dying seal, but as he stood over it, he had no answers. It certainly didn't look like anything he'd ever seen and, if anything, it had the shape of the sort of creature his son might have looked at in prehistory books at school. Approximately 5 feet (1.5 meters) in length, with a round body, long tail, and neck supporting a small head, it certainly looked like fabled images of underwater creatures such as the Loch Ness monster—or the legendary Altamaha-ha, or "Alty."

Warren quickly realized he might have stumbled upon something more than just newsworthy, took out his cell phone, and videoed and photographed the carcass, before sending the images to the nearby *Savannah Morning News* with a message, "This isn't a joke." The problem was, other wildlife was just as curious about the shore's new decaying—and possibly tasty—treasure as Warren and the media outlets he was now contacting. A local heron had already shown a keen interest in the mystery animal and other birds were keen to peck away at the salty snack. By the time experts arrived, the birds and the tide had taken the remains to a watery and permanent grave, so all they had to go on was Warren's phone. The immediate reaction was that the "creature" was a hoax, some sort of model. Warren disagreed, but the biologists remained unconvinced.

Above: The most typical descriptions are of an animal with an almost sturgeon-like body, a snout resembling that of an alligator, large protruding eyes, and many sharp white teeth.

"I am convinced the 'sea creature' is a constructed model of a baby Altamaha-ha monster," said John Crawford, a naturalist at the University of Georgia. Quinton White, a marine biologist from Jacksonville University, was a little blunter: "That could easily be faked. I think someone's playing a joke on us," he said. The fact that the creature was found in the exact stretch of water that the Altamaha-ha legend was born, and over years took shape, interested many, but only convinced the scientists that someone, with the legendary animal in mind, had played a hoax.

If it was a model, though, why were the birds having a nibble? The legend continues. If you find yourself on the shores of the Altamaha River, remember to keep an eye out. You might not be alone…

— ALTERNATIVE —
THEORIES

Similarities between the Altamaha-ha monster and that of the Loch Ness variety are striking. The shape of the mystery creatures is very close, as is the way it swims. Cynics will point to history here and the fact that many of the first settlers in the area came from Inverness in the 1700s. Inverness is a Scottish city near Loch Ness, and for many who made the journey to the New World, keeping hold of old, familiar myths would have soothed their understandable homesickness. Whether they ever heard the stories of that snake-like creature, as described by Native Americans in the area, we may never know.

Of the washed-up creature filmed in 2018, many experts thought it might be a deep-sea shark such as the frilled shark. The lack of gills confused many but decomposition could explain their absence. Other theories regarding the historical sightings of the animal point to the alligator gar, a large fish known to live in the area and described by any as a "living fossil" due to it retaining some morphological characteristics of its ancestors, including the ability to breathe both on land and underwater.

Below: There are striking similarities between Nessie and Alty—are they living legends or living fossils?

ENIGMATIC PEOPLE

In the modern world identities have never been so public and on display; whether we are on social media, browsing the Internet, or on our cell phones, we are constantly connected. In both the distant and recent past it was easier to remain hidden, and for your entire identity to remain a secret. This chapter looks at those people who became enigmas, and managed to keep their names and stories firmly in the dark.

There was Leatherman, who walked a continuous 365-mile loop through the countryside of Connecticut and New York state for more than three decades in the late nineteenth century, clad in a leather hat, jacket, and pants. He became a minor celebrity, but no one ever confirmed his name, where he came from, or why he made this walk dressed in leather. Nearly half a century after Norwegian police discovered the burned remains of a woman's body on rocks in the Isdalen Valley, they are no nearer to establishing just who she was. She has become known as the Isdal Woman, and the source of much fascination, but her true identity, and why she was killed, remains a mystery. And during World War II a group of boys discovered the body of a woman inside a tree in woods in England, but, once again, who she was has never been confirmed; and she has simply become known as "Bella in the Wych Elm."

Left: What truth lay hidden behind the iron mask of Louis XIV's most famous prisoner?

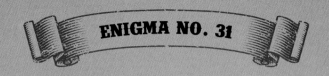

ENIGMA NO. 31

WHO WERE THE GREEN CHILDREN OF WOOLPIT?

Date: 1135–1154
Location: Woolpit, Suffolk, England

On a summer's day during the reign of King Stephen, the people of Woolpit, a village in Suffolk in the east of England, known for creating pits to capture wolves, discovered a boy and a girl standing by one of the pits.

The pair were brother and sister, and appeared to be normal children but for the color of their skin, which was a strange green. "The color of their skin differed from all mortals of our habitable world," wrote a monk by the name of Ralph of Coggeshall some years later. "For the whole surface of their skins was tinged with a green color." They could not speak English or communicate with the confused villagers, but instead spoke to each other in a language no one else could understand. The villagers took in these lost children, and soon learned they would only eat raw broad beans. In time, they would learn to eat other foods, and the green tinge of their skin faded.

Above: Could a diet of raw broad beans really turn you green?

A TALE TO TELL

The boy became sick and weak and would die not long after his arrival in the village, but the girl would go on to lead a long life in the area. Once she had learned to speak English, she would later explain the events that brought them to Woolpit. According to Ralph of Coggeshall's account, she said she and her brother had lived in what could only be described as another world, where everything and everybody was green, and where the sun never rose in the sky and they existed in a permanent twilight. The girl said they could also see another land across the river.

Another monk, William of Newburgh, also covered this mysterious event years later, and said that the children claimed to have come from a place called St. Martin. One day, the children were herding their father's cows and sheep near a cave, when they suddenly heard the sound of bells, which lured them to investigate. William of Newburgh stated he believed these bells were from nearby Bury St. Edmunds.

One source for Ralph of Coggeshall's story is Sir Richard de Calne of Wykes, who allowed the children to live with him in his manor, where the girl, once she had adjusted to her new life, would become a servant for many years. She would go on to marry a man from neighboring Norfolk, who is believed to have been Richard Barre, an ambassador of King Henry II. The astronomer and writer Duncan Lunan looked into Richard de Calne's family history and determined that the girl was called Agnes.

FOLKLORE OR FACT?

Some of the villagers believed that the children had been poisoned with arsenic, which can turn the skin green, by a guardian who had left them to die so that he could take their money. More likely, it is thought that the color of the children's skin was due to chlorosis (hypochromic anemia), which derives from the Greek word *chloris*, meaning a blend of green and yellow. A poor diet can cause this condition and a symptom is the skin turning a shade of green. So, who were the children, and where did they come from?

The most believable account is that they were Flemish orphans, who stumbled into the village fresh from a battle. In 1173 the Battle of Fornham between Henry II and Robert de Beaumont saw many Flemish immigrants killed at their settlement near the village of Fornham St. Martin, Suffolk. The children could have witnessed their parents being killed and fled to Thetford Forest (the "twilight world"). In this area at the time there were also several underground mine passages, which the children could have wandered through ("a cave").

Below: Today, Woolpit hosts a sign in the center of the village featuring an image of the two children, but nearly 900 years later, who they were and where they came from remains unsolved.

— ALTERNATIVE —
THEORIES

In the years since the children arrived, it has been speculated that they were from another world—aliens or extraterrestrials who came to Earth. In 1621 Robert Burton wrote in his book *The Anatomy of Melancholy* that the children "fell from Heaven." It was a theory expanded upon in 1996, when the astronomer Duncan Lunan suggested the children arrived in the village by mistake from another planet. Their home was trapped in an area beyond the Sun, forcing them to live in a dark twilight zone. Their green skin, so the theory goes, was caused by eating genetically modified plants on their planet.

Below: Were the children Flemish orphans, or extraterrestrials who fell from the skies?

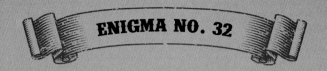

WHO WAS THE MAN BEHIND THE IRON MASK?

Date: 1669–1703
Location: France

The subject of many books, historical studies, and Hollywood movies, the mystery of the identity of "the Man in the Iron Mask" has never been solved.

Long before the strange prisoner's death in 1703, rumor and intrigue had gripped France regarding the true identity of a mystery that would, in time, be known as the Man in the Iron Mask. What was known back then was that a man had been imprisoned at the request of Louis XIV, France's ruler. When details emerged that the prisoner had been forced to wear a mask to hide his face and, therefore, his true identity, gossip and legends emerged that over the centuries still inspire people to guess at the truth. Many historians, authors, and even modern filmmakers have given their versions of the events, but we may never know who was really behind the mask.

The earliest record of the prisoner's plight is from late July 1669. In a letter sent from the Marquis de Louvois, a minister of Louis XIV, to Bénigne Dauvergne de Saint-Mars, governor of Pignerol prison near Turin (then part of France), it was said that Saint-Mars would soon be receiving a new prisoner. It was requested that a special cell be prepared, one with double doors—to prevent people listening in—and that Saint-Mars should see the prisoner only once a day to provide food; should the prisoner speak of anything other than what he needed, he was to be killed. Legend has it that this prisoner was always hidden beneath a mask.

Below: Voltaire wrote that, with the exception of the mask, the prisoner was treated well when at the Bastille, and this historic print supports his account.

A HARSH NEW HOME

The prison at Pignerol was a harsh place, reserved for men considered an embarrassment to the king, and it housed only a handful of inmates at a time. Other inmates in those years of the mystery prisoner were said to be: Count Ercole Antonio Mattioli, an Italian diplomat accused of double-crossing the French over the sale of a fortress town near the Franco-Italian border; Nicolas Fouquet, a former superintendent of finances, imprisoned for embezzlement; and the Marquis de Lauzun, who had become engaged to the king's cousin without his consent.

Above: The iron mask was sighted several times on the journey from Pignerol to Sainte-Marguerite prison (above), on a small island just a mile off the Mediterranean coast near Cannes.

Pignerol was infamous for its hard way of life. Secluded and bleak, the former fortress had gained notoriety for being the most feared of France's many prisons, a place Louis XIV chose personally to send men he deemed most deserving of its harsh walls. There would be no visitors, no contact with other inmates, no reading, and no exercise.

A DIVISIVE RULER

Each man stood accused of disappointing the king. Louis XIV himself divided opinion. To admirers and supporters, he was the *Roi Soleil* (the Sun King), a man of substance and strength, and France, under his reign, had grown in both stature and territory. Those who cared less for him spoke of a tyrant, a man who believed in absolutism and the notion that he acted as God's representative on Earth. Such was this conviction, according to those who disliked him and his reign, that France had become a police state.

In 1681 Saint-Mars was appointed governor of the Exilles Fort in what is now Italy, and it was decreed that the mysterious prisoner was to move with him. The same thing happened again six years later when Saint-Mars was to take over at Sainte-Marguerite prison, on the Mediterranean coast. It was on that journey that rumor began to spread that the prisoner in the constant charge of Saint-Mars did in fact wear a mask. The two men stayed in Sainte-Marguerite for only a year before Saint-Mars became governor of the Bastille prison in Paris. An official there wrote in his memoirs of a prisoner, "who is always masked and whose name is never pronounced." It was here that the prisoner died. Buried immediately in the Saint-Paul cemetery in the French capital under the name of "Marchioly," all of his clothing and furniture was destroyed, while his cell was whitewashed, and any metal possessions melted down. It was said that the deceased was in his fifties—strange given that he had apparently been sentenced nearly 35 years before.

A LITERARY FIGURE

It was the French writer and philosopher Voltaire—himself imprisoned at the Bastille, where he had been told about the mystery man by old inmates—who, in 1771, wrote of the events, and it is he who suggested that the mask worn by the mystery man was made of iron. Wardens at the Bastille had talked of a mask made of cloth, similar to the velvet masks worn by continental women to keep the sun from damaging their faces. Voltaire wrote of an "unknown prisoner, of majestic height, young, of a graceful and noble figure," probably of a regal background, as his manners were refined, and who played the guitar. He was served fine food, kept away from any contact with the other prisoners, and was only visited by the governor. Other writers, notably Alexandre Dumas in the 1840s, wrote extensively of the prisoner in the mask, prompting many other books and Hollywood movies that to try and convey the life and mystery of the prisoner.

Below: The prisoner seems to have been under the guardianship of Bénigne Dauvergne de Saint-Mars, governor of Pignerol and then the Bastille.

Historians continue to this day to try to explain events, and a recent study gave the name Eustache Dauger as a likely candidate. Dauger was a man of little means, arrested in 1669 for an unknown crime. It is said that the letter first received by Saint-Mars from Louvois mentioned the name Dauger and that he became the valet of Fouquet, another inmate, and may have been privy to confidential information about France, hence the mask and the seclusion. Many others dispute the recent findings, arguing that the name was merely a pseudonym. Instead, they point to centuries of differing theories. It seems the mystery of the Man in the Iron Mask is set to run.

— ALTERNATIVE —
THEORIES

Voltaire, when writing about the legend in 1771, argued the prisoner was in fact the older, illegitimate brother of Louis XIV, born from an affair between Anne of Austria and Cardinal Mazarin. Others also believe it was the King's brother, and Dumas himself, in his novels, depicted the prisoner as Louis' twin brother. Many historians have studied whether there was a twin and the possibility of a dispute over which child had been born first, and was therefore heir to the French throne.

Above: Did the King's own son— depicted here being arrested— reside behind the iron mask?

In France at the time, the royal court was awash with rumor, usually focusing on the large royal family. The king's son, Louis de Bourbon, had been banished for being outed as a homosexual. He tried to regain favor by fighting in the campaign in Flanders, where it is said he died. However, others suggested that he had instead been banished to prison, and concealed behind the mask.

Other theories point to a French general named Vivien de Bulonde, imprisoned for withdrawing troops from the Siege of Cuneo and abandoning wounded servicemen. Another argument, first made by the English politician Hugh Cecil, was that the prisoner was the king's father, Louis XIII, stating that at the king's birth, his father had been estranged from his mother for many years, and his real father had been sent away, masked for the rest of his life.

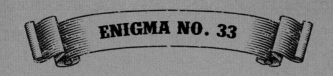

WHO WAS BEETHOVEN'S "IMMORTAL BELOVED"?

Date: 1812
Location: Teplice, Czech Republic

The revered German composer Ludwig van Beethoven once wrote a letter to his "Immortal Beloved." The letter was seemingly never sent, and the identity of his beloved has baffled scholars for 200 years.

Ludwig van Beethoven, composer and pianist, was one of the greatest musicians to put notes to paper. Among his many lauded musical feats, Beethoven is seen as a crucial pioneer in the development of classical music's Romantic era. In 1810, at the height of Beethoven's fame, the German Romantic author E. T. A. Hoffmann wrote about him in the same breath as Mozart and Joseph Haydn, calling them, "the three masters of instrumental compositions," who "breathe one and the same Romantic spirit." Beethoven had been heavily influenced by Mozart and had met and learned from Haydn, his music becoming famous all over Europe, but for all the romance and passion that his musical talents gave the world, his own love life was by no means a symphony.

Right: For a man credited as one of the pioneers of the Romantic era, Beethoven's own love life was thwarted at many turns.

The composer did find romance—and even love—but he was hindered by position and status. Born in Bonn, Germany, in late 1770, Beethoven, the son of a musician, was a promising young pianist who moved to Vienna to start a career in music at the age of 22. It was here that he first studied with Haydn, before having his first mature work published in 1795. He would remain living in Vienna, unmarried, until his death in 1827.

UNLUCKY IN LOVE

As well as composing pieces of music that have endured for over two centuries, the young man would teach, mainly within high circles, and it was in these regal homes that Beethoven met and fell in love with a number of women—often his students, whose aristocratic positions contrasted with his own status as a commoner, which meant that even when his love was requited, the romance could never be allowed to blossom.

In 1801 Beethoven started to teach Giulietta Guicciardi, an Austrian countess, for whom his affections were made clear in a letter to a childhood friend. Given their different positions in life, he could never take this love further. Instead he wrote Piano Sonata No.14 (the *Moonlight Sonata*) and dedicated it to her.

Beethoven had met Guicciardi through his relationship with the Von Brunsvik family and especially Countess Jozefina, whom he also taught piano and for whom he had also developed strong feelings. Jozefina had been married to Count Joseph Deym, but upon his death in 1804, her relationship with the famous composer deepened, which was underlined by a series of letters written to her by Beethoven in which he declared his love for her. Once again, though, the object of this passion was forbidden: this time the countess's family, in 1807, insisted she withdraw from him; three years later she married the Baron von Stackelberg. That same year it is thought that Beethoven himself had proposed unsuccessfully to Therese Malfatti, a musician in Vienna, but, being the daughter of a wealthy merchant, Beethoven was again scorned. He turned once more to his music; this time dedicating his famous piece *Für Elise* to her.

Below: It is thought that despite Therese Malfatti spurning Beethoven's love, he dedicated one of his most famous pieces to her.

Above: The letter was written in the spa town of Teplice, where Beethoven was twice sent for convalescence.

COMPOSING HIS LETTER

In 1811, while his heart may have been broken, a high fever and headaches saw Beethoven taken to the Czech spa town of Teplice, and, while he recovered in time to write his seventh symphony the following winter, his ill health returned, and he was ordered by his doctor to spend the summer of 1812 back in Teplice. It was there, convalescing, that he wrote his letter, addressing it to his "Immortal Beloved."

Written on 10 small pages, in pencil and in three parts, Beethoven's letter speaks to a lady for whom he clearly had a deep love. "My angel, my all, my own self," he wrote. "Can our love persist otherwise than through sacrifices, than by not demanding everything? Canst thou change it, that thou art not entirely mine, I not entirely thine?" He continued, "Though still in bed, my thoughts go out to you, my Immortal Beloved. Be calm—love me—today—yesterday—what tearful longings for you—you—you—my life—my all—farewell. Oh continue to love me—never misjudge the most faithful heart of your beloved. Ever thine. Ever mine. Ever ours."

It is not known why the letter was never sent; it was only discovered in Beethoven's estate after his death in 1827 by his secretary Anton Schindler, who kept it in his possession before leaving it in his will to his sister, who, in turn, in 1880 sold it to the Berlin State Library, where it resides to this day. The letter was never dated and gave no indication of where Beethoven had written it, but in the 1950s, with analysis of the watermark, the date was discovered, and, from other kept correspondence, the mystery of his whereabouts was solved.

Above: One page of the 10-page letter that was written with such passion and yet never sent.

What wasn't solved—and still intrigues scholars today—is whom the great composer was writing to, whom those "tearful longings" were for, and for which of the many women in his life he had these feelings: Who was his "Immortal Beloved"?

— ALTERNATIVE —
THEORIES

Since Beethoven's death in 1827 and the discovery of his letter, friends and scholars have pondered the identity of his penned passion. Popular in Vienna, the composer met many women, and theories have varied. Viennese pianist Dorothea von Ertmann was very close to Beethoven, as was the German writer and novelist Bettina von Arnim. Both have been proposed as would-be recipients, but, as the years have passed, there are three ladies thought more likely to be the object of Beethoven's desires.

Antonie Brentano was an Austrian patron of the arts and, in 1812, the year Beethoven wrote the letter, lived in the same hotel as Beethoven. It is known they were close, and he did write to her, but he was friendly with her husband, which suggests the relationship was platonic. The spotlight also shines on the Brunsvik family. Therese was a student of the composer and a recipient of a dedicated piano sonata (No. 24) that Beethoven nicknamed *à Thérèse*.

Above: Did Beethoven fall in love with sisters, and ultimately express his desire for the younger of the two, Jozefina?

The countess's diary entries talk of a deep regard for Beethoven, and they did write to each other, often romantically. It is, though, these very diary entries that point to her younger sibling, Jozefina. In one extract, Therese asks why, as a widow, doesn't her sister take Beethoven as a husband, calling him "Jozefina's soul-mate." It is Jozefina, then, who most scholars believe to be Beethoven's beloved, but it seems the world will never know for sure.

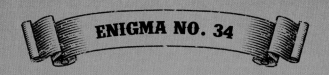

WHY DID LEATHERMAN WALK?

Date: ca. 1857–1889
Location: Connecticut and New York

In the nineteenth century, a man dressed in leather walked continuously through the American countryside, but it has never been established who he was, or why he was doing it.

From around 1857 until 1889, a mysterious figure clad head-to-toe in leather walked a circuit of 365 miles (585 kilometers) through Connecticut and New York state, which he would complete precisely every 34 days, whatever the weather. Leatherman would walk between the Connecticut and Hudson Rivers, from Saybrook to Greenwich, then inland and on a loop through towns such as Ossining, Yorktown, North Salem, Bridgewater, Forestville, and New Britain.

"The first time I saw him walking through my parents' farm I was a very small boy," Walter Whitson has recalled. "He scared the life out of me and I began to run for all I was worth." A strange-looking character, Leatherman's leather suit made him look larger than he was and gave him an uncomfortable gait.

He was also largely silent: he didn't speak to those he passed, and, if he needed to communicate, he would do so with grunts and hand gestures. Those who attempted to speak with him can only recall him using a few words in broken English.

A LOCAL CELEBRITY

Over time, Leatherman would grow less scary and be embraced by local communities, who grew accustomed to seeing him walk through their towns. He would knock on the back doors of houses and ask for a meal, but not with words—rather by pointing to his mouth. He would be served a meal outside and then be on his way with possibly only a bow, a grunt, or nothing at all. And then, 34 days later, he would knock at the same house for another

meal. Without fail it was every 34 days later, time and time again. These houses knew exactly when to expect him.

Above: Leatherman wore a unique handmade outfit, which consisted of a large leather coat, leather trousers, leather boots, and a leather hat perched on his head.

"People would mark on their calendars when to expect the Leatherman; they would even miss the Sunday school picnic, so they could be there to feed him," Sarah Foot, who interviewed many people who met Leatherman, has said. "They would bake hot biscuits especially for him and have them waiting for him. These people liked the Leatherman, because they enjoyed doing something kind for someone else."

Leatherman became something of a local celebrity, and communities would watch him walk through their town. Some treated him with more distrust and suspicion; in New Haven the locals attempted to get him drunk to get him to talk more, and in Forestville he was pushed over. To avoid potentially threatening encounters, Leatherman would try to stick to country roads where the locals were usually friendlier, and would greet him and even offer him a place to stay. He always declined, and instead would spend each night in shelters made of rocks. To keep warm, he would make a campfire and indulge his one great pleasure, smoking tobacco from a handmade pipe. Sometimes, local children would sit with him, but there was no conversation. Just the crackle of the fire.

MEETING HIS END

Leatherman managed to live outside for all those years, although many assumed that the famous blizzard of 1888 would claim him. He survived it, and was only delayed on his loop by four days. Toward the end of that same year, the Humane Society had him arrested and taken to a hospital so that a sore on his face could be treated. It was found to be cancer, but Leatherman managed to escape the confines of the hospital and returned to his route.

Below: Some of the "Leatherman caves"— rock shelters in the forest—still stand today, and one became the wanderer's final shelter.

On March 24, 1889, Leatherman's body was discovered in one of his rock shelters in Saw Mill wood, on the farm of George Dell in Mount Pleasant, New York. He had died of his cancer. On the day he was buried, he commanded front-page obituaries in the *New York Sun* and *Hartford Times*. Leatherman was buried in Sparta Cemetery next to a road, but his followers campaigned for a more appropriate and peaceful burial site, which was granted in May 2011. However, when his original coffin was dug out, all that was found was some dirt and nails; there was no body or bones to test for DNA. The dirt and nails were placed in a new plain pine coffin and buried at a new site at Ossining, New York. His tombstone simply reads "The Leatherman."

ALTERNATIVE
THEORIES

So why did Leatherman live this life as a wandering hermit, and what was his true identity? In December 1888, the New York press reported that his name was Jules Bourglay, and that he was from Lyon in France, where he had grown up as the son of a carpenter. He had fallen in love with Margaret Laron, the daughter of a leather merchant, who agreed to marry him if he proved himself a success in her father's business. Leatherman made some poor investments and ultimately ruined the business, which would see the wedding canceled. He suffered a mental breakdown and was placed in a Paris hospital, only to escape and next be seen in the US, symbolically clad in leather.

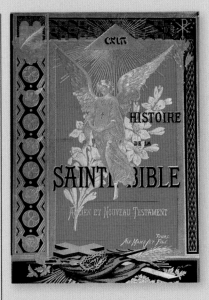

Above: A French prayer book supports the notion Leatherman was French, but it is still uncertain who he was.

Leatherman was deeply private, and never told anyone his name, or where he was from. He was first named as Jules Bourglay in a story in the *Waterbury Daily American* in August 1884, and this was the name on his first tombstone, but it was never confirmed, did not appear on his death certificate, and several researchers have tried but failed to confirm his true identity. However, there is good reason to believe that he was French, for he was fluent in the language, and a French prayer book was found among his possessions when his body was discovered.

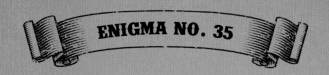

WHAT WAS THE STORY OF "JEROME" OF NOVA SCOTIA?

Date: 1863–1912
Location: Sandy Cove, Nova Scotia

Discovered alone, cold, and with both his legs amputated, a stranger was taken in by the local communities of Nova Scotia, Canada. His true identity has never been discovered.

On a cold September morning in 1863, an eight-year-old boy named George Colin Albright was combing the beach at Sandy Cove, near his home, when he made a strange discovery, one that would puzzle locals and the wider world. There, sitting near the shore, was a young man. He was sitting up, looking out to sea, with some bread and a jug next to him. Had he been there all night? He certainly seemed to be suffering the effects of being exposed to the night's chill, but as the boy got closer, he noticed the most striking thing about the strange visitor—both of his legs were missing.

The boy ran for help. He approached several adults but was unable to convince them of his discovery. Eventually two farmers listened and, seeing the genuine shock in the boy's eyes, they accompanied him back to the beach to find the man still there, but now, having used his arms, he had edged himself forward, closer to the shore. The men presumed he had suicide on his mind and quickly came to his aid, carrying him home to the young boy's parents' home in the nearby village of Digby Neck.

Above: A man with no legs is found on the beach at Sandy Cove, staring out to sea. And so the mystery begins…

Above: Jerome—
photographed here
for the *Daily Echo*,
April 20, 1912, Digby
County, Nova Scotia—
gave no indication of
where he came from
or what had happened
to him.

NURSED BACK TO HEALTH

The man would hardly communicate. When asked his name, a word resembling "Jerome" was uttered, and so the stranger was named. A doctor was sent for, who then examined the man. Suffering severely from exposure to the cold, the man could be treated, but the doctor was keen to know what had happened to his legs. He got no answers from his patient. On examination, though, the doctor could see that Jerome's legs had been amputated just above the knee, clearly by a qualified physician. The bandages were fresh and there was some bleeding. The surgery must have been quite recent.

Comfortable in the Albright home, Jerome became the talk of the village. Many came to take a look and to try and talk him into providing answers. They all failed. It wasn't clear whether he didn't understand English or simply didn't want to talk. One local tried to communicate in Latin, French, Italian, and Spanish, but nothing. In fact, once recovered from his hypothermia, Jerome could be quite aggressive to those who tried to get too close a look, even snarling at some like a dog. He did like children, though. Softening in their presence, he liked to play with them, but remained silent about his past and identity.

Visitors continued to come to the Albright home but were met only by Jerome's continued aggression, leaving the villagers to speculate. Jerome's hands were too soft to suggest he was a manual laborer. He had a Mediterranean look about him, and they therefore presumed he was a Catholic. Priests were sent for, as were other clergy, but none could coax any further information from him. Newspaper men came, too—the story started to spread, and soon the whole state of Nova Scotia was aware of the new mystery resident.

JEROME ON THE MOVE

The Albright home had been a welcoming one, but the young boy's father was a fisherman, and another mouth to feed was taking its toll. The fact that the people of Digby Neck had concluded that their guest was a Catholic would dictate Jerome's next move. The villagers were Baptists, so they suggested moving him to the nearby French community of Meteghan. There he moved in with Jean Nicola, a Corsican deserter, known as "the Russian" due to his time fighting in the Crimea. Jean had a family. His wife, Juliette, and his stepdaughter liked Jerome; he was sweet to them but was more aggressive and at odds with the man of the house. Like the Albrights, Jean now had another mouth to feed, but by now the government of Nova Scotia had intervened and decreed that $2 a week should be made available for the upkeep of Jerome.

When Juliette died, Nicola returned to Europe and so Jerome moved in with the Comeau family, where his $2 weekly allowance was topped up further by paying visitors keen to see the man with no background, no legs, and no voice.

Below: The Baptist villagers of Digby Neck thought it better to move the presumed Catholic visitor to a nearby French community.

A FEW CLUES

Jerome's supposed lack of voice wasn't entirely true. While most happy when playing with the Comeau children, he had communicated that he had been on a boat called the *Columbo* and that

Left: Could it be that "Jerome" was just one of the many wounded soldiers of the Civil War?

Right: Did "Jerome" in fact lose his legs to gangrene after falling through ice?

he might have originally been from the Adriatic coast of Italy. Fascinated onlookers believed they were visiting a disgraced member of a European royal family, a myth the Comeaus were never going to rubbish, not when it brought in paying visitors. Others talked of the American Civil War, which was raging in the United States at the time, and presumed that here was a wounded officer, traumatized by battle.

On one occasion, two women arrived at the Comeau home and asked to see Jerome alone. Inside his room, they spoke quietly and it was unsure what their attentions were, but when leaving, they were heard to say, "He is well here. Let him be." Jerome was well in Meteghan. He lived out another 49 years after his discovery, and, while he continued to live with very limited speech and suffering from both anxiety and supposed depression, sometimes at night he could be heard singing in a language that no one could identify. On April 15, 1912, Jerome died. Strangely, it was the same day that the RMS *Titanic* went down. In Nova Scotia, there is a marked gravestone that simply reads "Jerome."

— ALTERNATIVE —
THEORIES

Speculation circled around Jerome for his known life and beyond his death. The stories of European royalty never went away, joined by talk of him being a mutinous sailor, punished for his rebellion with amputation. Others concocted a story of Jerome as the heir to a huge fortune, mutilated by a family member and left on the shore.

What has more credence is the story that in 1859, just three years before Jerome's arrival in Sandy Cove, a young foreign man fell through ice in New Brunswick, across the Bay of Fundy. Gangrene set into his legs and both were amputated. The man was known as Gamby (*gambe* being Italian for a leg) but being a burden to the community in New Brunswick, the man was put aboard a vessel and soon left by the ship's captain on the Sandy Cove beach where he became Nova Scotia's Jerome. This theory is seen by some as solving the long mystery; others have called it "speculative fiction."

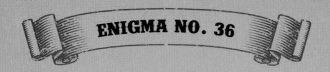

WHO PUT BELLA IN THE WYCH ELM?

Date: April 1943
Location: Hagley Wood, Worcestershire, England

The body of a woman is discovered inside the hollowed-out trunk of a tree during World War II, but who is she, and how did she get there?

As the sun set over Hagley Woods on April 18, 1943, four young boys—Thomas Willetts, Robert Hart, Bob Farmer, and Fred Payne—were out together looking for birds' nests and eggs when they came across a large wych elm tree with an intriguing hollow trunk. The smallest of the group, Farmer, volunteered to climb the tree, believing it would be a good place to find a bird's nest, when he peered inside the trunk and discovered a skull.

They were all adventurous boys, and, at first, none of them were scared, as they assumed it was just an animal's skull, but, on closer inspection, they could see human hair and teeth. The boys should not have even been there—they were trespassing on the Hagley Estate owned by Lord Cobham, and so they put the skull back where they found it and returned home, with a solemn promise to each other that they would not speak about their discovery to anyone. However, the youngest of the group, Willetts, felt uneasy at this pact of silence and soon told his father, who quickly informed Warwickshire Police.

RECOVERING THE REMAINS

The police and the Home Guard, with the assistance of a lumberjack who was needed to hack into the tree, recovered all the remains from inside the tree, as well as pieces of clothing. They found a skeleton, a shoe, and a gold wedding ring; some hair was sprouting from the top of the skull and the teeth were still in place. A piece of taffeta had been jammed into the mouth of the skull. There was no flesh at all. Near the tree, a skeletal hand was also found.

Pathologist professor James Webster, from the nearby University of Birmingham, believed that the skull had belonged to a woman who was aged around 35. She had probably been about 5 feet (1.5 meters) tall, and could have been a mother to one child, but that was not certain. Webster said the woman had been dead for at least 18 months, so from the end of 1941, and she had been placed in the tree while she was still alive or just after she had been killed: a body stiffened with rigor mortis would have been unable to fit inside the tree. She had been suffocated with the piece of taffeta found inside her mouth. Any future tests would be rendered impossible, as both the bones and the forensic files would soon be misplaced by the University of Birmingham. They have never been found.

Above: The pathologist thought the woman was put in the hollow when she was still alive or recently deceased.

To begin with, the police waded through the files of missing persons—as this was wartime there were many—but they came up with nothing. They also approached dentists across the country to see if they could find a match for the skeleton's teeth, but again, nothing.

Six months after the discovery of the remains in the tree, with the trail having gone cold, a piece of graffiti appeared on a wall in Upper Dean Street in Birmingham, which read: "Who put Bella down the Wych Elm, Hagley Wood?" The message would be repeated on other walls throughout the area. Suddenly the police had a name to help with their enquiries, as someone clearly knew the identity of the victim and could offer some leads, but they had no joy in finding out either who had produced the graffiti or who Bella was.

Below: The Wychbury Obelisk, built in the 1740s, on Wychbury Hill, Hagley Park, has been graffitied in the style of the original graffiti that supplied the police with a name.

Above: Had "Bella" been the girlfriend of the last man executed at the Tower of London, Josef Jakobs?

A WITCH OR A SPY?

There had long been speculation that covens of witches would meet in Hagley Wood, and in 1945, Margaret Murray, an anthropologist and archaeologist at University College London, suggested Bella had been killed and her hand removed during an occult ceremony. Murray's fascination with witches was not enough, and she failed to provide any credible evidence.

In 1953, the *Wolverhampton Express and Star* was contacted by a reader who believed that Bella's full name was Clarabella Dronkers, and that she was a spy who had been sent by the Germans to gather intelligence on the munitions factories in the West Midlands during the war. Bella was part of a wider spy ring consisting of a Dutchman, a trapeze artist, and a British Army officer who was spying for the Germans, but when she learned too much she was killed by two others in the ring and her body taken to Hagley Woods. The reader was a friend of the trapeze artist and was passing along the information in confidence to the newspaper. The police looked into it but found little else to go on.

As Bella had been killed in 1941, there was a refusal to believe it was a simple case of murder; it was thought that her death must be connected to the war. In that year, Czech-born Gestapo agent Josef Jakobs had parachuted into Cambridgeshire, breaking his ankle on landing and being arrested by the Home Guard. He would become the last man to be executed at the Tower of London when he faced a firing squad in August 1941. When arrested, Jakobs was carrying a photograph of his girlfriend, the German singer and actress Clara Bauerle, who he claimed was also a spy for the Nazis, and was due to come to England, too. However, he had not been able to radio her before his capture.

Clara Bauerle was 35 and spoke English, as she had worked in the music halls of the West Midlands before the outbreak of war, and so it is easy to understand how her name became slightly mangled and remembered as Clarabella or Bella. Could Bauerle be the victim of the wych tree? She had been due to parachute into the Midlands in 1941, the year of the death in question, and afterward there appears to be no trace of her back in Germany—no more appearances, no more singing dates, movies, or recordings. The case weakened when it was determined that there was no evidence Bauerle was in England in 1941, and standing at 6 feet (1.8 meters) tall, she was a foot taller than Bella was estimated to be. In September 2016 it was also discovered that she had died in Berlin in December 1942.

If not Bauerle, then other theories have suggested the remains belonged to a prostitute called Bella who worked on the nearby Hagley Road—a local girl who was murdered when she became pregnant by an American soldier—or a woman who had sheltered there from a German air raid and become stuck.

Right: Even the retrieval of the skull failed to provide a firm identification of the wych elm victim.

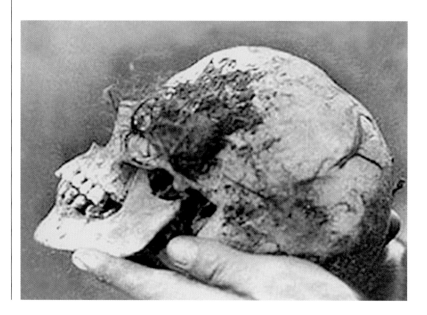

ALTERNATIVE
THEORIES

In 1953 Una Mossop came forward and told the police that her former husband, Jack Mossop, had put Bella in the tree, along with a Dutchman named Van Ralt, after a night out. The rather tenuous reason was that the woman had become drunk and they placed her in the tree to sober her up and stop her drinking. It transpired that Jack Mossop had mental health problems and was sectioned in Stafford Mental Hospital, complaining about seeing a woman staring at him from a tree. He died before the body was found, and his ex-wife Una waited another decade after the discovery of the body to come forward to the police, and so she was inevitably treated as an unreliable witness.

Above: A man in a mental institution complains of seeing a woman staring at him from a tree; his wife says he is the prime suspect.

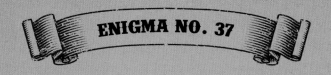

WHO WAS THE BABUSHKA LADY?

Date: November 22, 1963
Location: Dallas, Texas

As gunshots echoed around Dealey Plaza, chaos ensued. Huge crowds had come to catch a glimpse of their president, but now they ducked for cover. Except for one scarfed woman, who was caught on camera standing calmly, before slowly walking away.

Of all the enigmatic events that have dotted the history books over the centuries, none have caused more intrigue or sheer speculation than the 1963 assassination of John F. Kennedy. Conspiracy theories have flourished, while articles, books, and movies have been devoured by an eager public desperate to get to the truth. Did Lee Harvey Oswald act alone? Were the CIA involved? Or was it the Mafia? Over 50 years later, there are still more questions than answers. One question that won't go away is the identity of one lady caught on many camera reels on that fateful day, a woman who stood amid all the panic after the shooting and apparently filmed her own version of events. She then left, but was never traced and nor was her footage.

John F. Kennedy had agreed to visit Dallas in Texas five months before his death. Three years into his presidency, Kennedy took his wife Jackie on a trip he hoped would raise funds and support for the following year's presidential campaign. He also hoped to heal rifts within his party in Texas, in dispute about whether Kennedy and his vice president, Lyndon B. Johnson, a Texan himself, were the right combination to fight and win the next election. Flights were planned, meetings set, lunches arranged, and the motorcade's route planned well in advance of being made public just days before the visit. The President and the First Lady arrived in the presidential aircraft Air Force One at a local airfield at 11:25 a.m., leaving 10 minutes later in a 1961 Lincoln Continental four-door convertible with the governor of Texas, John Connally, and his wife, Nellie. Due to the huge crowds, the presidential party were informed that their drive would take approximately 10 minutes longer than the scheduled 45 minutes.

Below: Prior to the assassination, President John F. Kennedy, First Lady Jacqueline Kennedy, and Texas governor John Connally ride through the streets of Dallas, Texas, on November 22, 1963.

The drive had gone well. Around 200,000 people were estimated to have lined the streets for their President and his wife. And then five minutes away from their destination, the motorcade turned left onto Dealey Plaza, slowly inching its way through the hordes. "Mr. President, you can't say that Dallas doesn't love you," Nellie Connally said, turning to face him in the car. "No, you certainly can't," said the President. They were his last words.

AN EERIE CALM

Moments later, shots rang out around the plaza—the number of shots would always be unclear, but what did become immediately apparent was that an assassination attempt on the president had been carried out and he had been hit.

Below: A pivotal and tragic scene in history unfolded here in Dallas, Texas. The Babushka Lady had a perfect view but never came forward to give evidence. Who was she, and where did she go?

 Original route

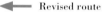 Revised route

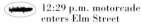 12:29 p.m. motorcade enters Elm Street

12:30 p.m. 3 bullets fired, president is hit

Babushka Lady

Umbrella Man

Badge Man

Main Street

Elm Street

Texas School Depository

Grassy knoll

Triple underpass

Colonnade

North Pergola

County Records

Dal-Tex Building

Dealey Plaza

Above: A Bell & Howell Model 414PD Director Series Zoomatic 8mm film camera was used for the Zapruder film, but failed to capture a clear view of the Babushka Lady's face.

Among the crowd, standing on the grass between Elm and Main Streets, was a woman. Caught on many films taken by those present that day, the lady was apparently filming the motorcade as it went by, but while most of her fellow onlookers dropped to take cover amid the chaos, she remained calm, and even moved closer to the motorcade and the dying president. The lady, caught from different angles, was wearing a long, tan coat, standing with a purposeful wide stance, and, most notably, was wearing a Russian headscarf, fashionable at the time and similar to those worn by Russian ladies, hence the label, the "Babushka Lady."

For the weeks and years that followed, plenty of those same onlookers spotted on film, or who filmed events themselves, would be given names by investigators. "Umbrella Man" and "Badge Man" were among those forthcoming with their evidence and footage, but it was the unknown whereabouts and subsequent movements of the lady with the scarf that frustrated those seeking the truth. Many studied the relevant footage, but even the most famous recording, known as the "Zapruder film," which is regarded as the most complete and was taken with a full-frontal view of the mysterious figure, is inconclusive, as she has what looks like a camera concealing her features.

After the shootings, the lady was spotted calmly moving away from the scene, making her way east on Elm Street, her identity lost among the panicked crowds. Her whereabouts, any footage she might have taken, and her name were never found. In March 1979 the Photographic Evidence Panel on the House Select Committee on assassinations brought up the enigmatic witness when it spoke of the importance of materials found that day, but, "Committee investigators located many of the suggested films and photographs, however, some items were never located, i.e., The Babushka Lady."

A SOLUTION REJECTED

In 1970 a former dancer named Beverly Oliver came forward, claiming to be the elusive witness to the world's most famous crime. Her claims were taken seriously enough to be investigated by the FBI, but when she said she was 17 years old at the time of the assassination (the original lady had seemed far older than that) and that she had filmed everything on a Yashica Super 8 camera (a model that was not produced until years after Kennedy's death), her story was rejected.

Half a century on and the assassination of President Kennedy on that sunny November lunchtime in Dallas still dominates a nation's psyche. One day, the skeptics believe, the truth will come out and we will know who shot JFK. Will we ever, though, know the identity of the Babushka Lady?

Below: Clearly shown on the right in this photograph, the Babushka Lady might have answered a lot of questions, had she ever been found.

ALTERNATIVE THEORIES

Many people have had their say on the identification of the Babushka Lady. The footage taken by others there that day portrays a well-built lady, and there are those who believe the mysterious person was in fact a man. That would explain the scarf. While it rained on the morning of the assassination, the early afternoon was dry and fine, and there was no need to cover the head. Others believe she was a Russian spy or assassin, with a gun disguised as a camera held at her face to conceal her features. Then there is the idea that she was a secret service agent involved in a government conspiracy to kill the country's president. Less sinister

Above: If the Babushka Lady was using binoculars, it would explain why she never came forward with any footage.

theories suggest that the lady was simply a relaxed onlooker, not scared by the shots around her or the bloody scene she was witnessing, and that in her hands, covering her face, was in fact a pair of binoculars, which is why no footage was ever found. What we may never know is why this woman—so talked about and pondered by those with a keen interest in the events of November 22, 1963—never came forward.

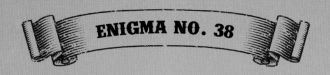

WHY HASN'T THE ISDAL WOMAN BEEN IDENTIFIED?

Date: November 29, 1970
Location: Norway

On the morning of November 29, 1970, a man and his two daughters hiking in the Isdalen Valley discovered the body of a woman wedged between a cluster of rocks.

It soon became clear this was not a simple case of a fellow hiker having fallen tragically to her death. The woman had been set on fire, and the first police on the scene recall a strong smell of burned flesh hanging in the air. The Bergen police also found a watch, an umbrella, jewelry, and some empty bottles among the rocks, but rather than being strewn all around, they had been placed next to the body. The labels on the bottles had been removed and the labels from the woman's clothes had also been cut out. It was impossible to identify the body, and so a public appeal was launched for a woman the police believed to be aged between 25 and 40, 5 feet 4 inches (1.63 meters) tall, and with brown or black hair. She would soon become known as the "Isdal Woman," an increasingly elusive and ghostlike figure as the Bergen police struggled to ascertain who she was and how she died.

Body found
in this area, wedged
between rocks

THE SUITCASES

The first breakthrough in the investigation came when it was discovered that the woman had left two suitcases in the left-luggage department at Bergen's railroad station. Inside one case, a pair of glasses was found that bore a fingerprint matching those of the victim. It was packed alongside some clothes, wigs, a hairbrush, teaspoons, eczema cream, 500 German marks, and 130 Norwegian kroner, as well as Belgian, Swiss, and British coins. To the police's great frustration, there was still nothing that revealed exactly who the woman was. There was a postcard from an Italian photographer who had taken her out for dinner; however, when questioned, he claimed that the woman had said she was an antiques dealer from South Africa.

Above: The body was found in the Isdalen Valley, on the west coast of Norway; Bergen can be seen in the distance.

One of the most useful pieces of evidence found in the suitcases was a plastic bag from Oscar Rortvedt's shoe store in Stavanger, 130 miles (210 kilometers) south of Bergen on the Norwegian coast. The police traveled to the store and interviewed the owner's son Rolf, who remembered selling a pair of rubber boots, which were found on the body, to a well-dressed woman with dark hair, who spoke some English and smelled of garlic. A woman matching this description had stayed at the St. Svithun Hotel in Stavanger for nine nights between November 9 and 18, 1970, checking out 11 days before the body was discovered. She had checked into the hotel as Fenella Lorch, but that was not her real name.

The police would soon learn that the same woman had stayed in nine different hotels in four Norwegian cities—Bergen, Stavanger, Trondheim, and Oslo—between March 21 and November 23, 1970, while using eight different aliases. At that time in Norway, a passport was required to check into a hotel, and so the woman would have had to use up to eight false passports with these aliases.

In the suitcases, the police had also found a piece of paper with what appeared to be a code written in blue ink, which they would soon decipher as a record of the woman's travels written in an abbreviated form of letters and numerals, in an attempt to disguise her movements.

THE ISDAL WOMAN'S MOVEMENTS BEFORE HER DEATH

Known route
—— *Basel to Stavanger*

Traveling between hotels
—— *March*
—— *October–November*

Above: This map tracks the Isdal Woman's known route through Europe (brown) and the traveling she did between hotels (pink and green) in the months leading up to her death.

Staff at the hotels could recall an elegant and sophisticated woman who was alone but would often ask to change her room. "Other than in magazines and movies, [she was] the kind of woman we never saw," Frank Ove Sivertsen, a bellboy at the Hotel Neptune in Bergen, told NRK, Norway's public radio service. The last sighting of the woman before her death was on November 23, when she paid her bill in cash, asked for a taxi to be ordered, and then checked out of the Hordaheimen Hotel in Bergen.

An autopsy found that the woman had been set on fire with the use of gasoline, and the discovery of particles of smoke in her lungs suggested that she had been alive when it happened. There were also an estimated 50 to 70 Fenemal sleeping pills found in her stomach.

Below: The body was laid to rest in a zinc coffin that would not decompose, in an unmarked grave in Møllendal Cemetery.

In February 1971, with no firm leads, the case was closed, and the unknown woman was laid to rest. However, the police hoped that one day a member of her family would come forward, and so kept photographs of her funeral and buried her in a zinc coffin that would not decompose. The Isdal Woman has become one of Norway's most enduring mysteries.

THE TEETH

In 2016 the case was reopened when the woman's teeth and several of her vital organs, including her heart, lung, and liver, were discovered in storage at Haukeland University Hospital. It was possible, with the teeth and tissue samples, to build the woman's extended DNA profile, which indicated she was European.

Her distinctive teeth, which had fillings and several gold crowns, suggested she was not from Scandinavia, but instead had had this dental work performed in the Far East, Central or Southern Europe, or South America. An isotope test of her teeth also detected chemical traces that showed she had grown up in an area around the French–German border, while experts at the Karolinska Institute in Sweden used the teeth to put her age at between 36 and 44 when she died.

In May 2017 the Norwegian police, armed with these new details, felt emboldened enough to issue an Interpol Black Notice for new information.

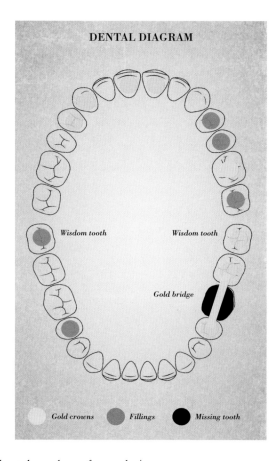

DENTAL DIAGRAM

Wisdom tooth   Wisdom tooth

Gold bridge

Gold crowns   Fillings   Missing tooth

Above: Discovered in storage at a university hospital, the mystery woman's teeth have renewed the search. The above diagram has been interpreted from the teeth found.

— ALTERNATIVE —
THEORIES

The false passports and mysterious movements of a woman so obviously keen to cover her tracks would appear to support the popular theory that she was a spy. However, Ornulf Tofte, the head of the Norwegian police security service, investigated whether she had been involved in espionage and found no evidence. However, this was at the height of the Cold War in the 1970s, and Norway was known to have spies traveling across the country. The security services in Norway had received reports the woman was indeed a spy and had been in the west of the country to watch the military test new rockets, but, again, this was never proven.

When the Bergen police closed the case for the first time, they officially ruled that the woman had probably committed suicide. However, taking a large number of sleeping pills and simultaneously setting yourself on fire seems an implausible way to kill yourself, while a bruise found on the side of the woman's neck suggested she could have been assaulted prior to her death.

Nearly half a century after her body was discovered, the identity of the Isdal Woman and how she met her death remain a mystery.

Below: Was the Isdal Woman sent to spy on the Norwegian military while they tested their new Penguin anti-ship missile?

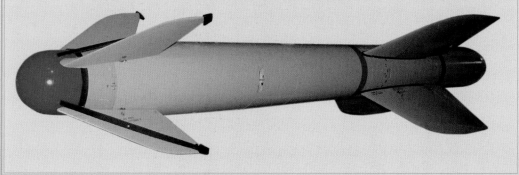

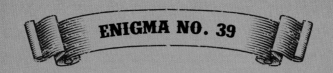

WHO WROTE THE CIRCLEVILLE LETTERS?

Date: 1976
Location: Circleville, Ohio

Anonymous letters being delivered to people's homes were disconcerting enough, but soon the letters became threatening, and, to this day, no one knows the true identity of the writer.

Circleville, Ohio, is a small town 25 miles (40 kilometers) south of Columbus. It is a quiet place, people know people, and nothing much happens. Until 1976, that is, when many of the town's 14,000 inhabitants started to receive strange anonymous letters in the mail. Some were lewd, some said very little at all, many contained very personal details. Most were opened and ignored.

Things took a more sinister turn when a local lady and school bus driver, Mary Gillespie, received a letter. Featuring no return address or signature, the letter stated that the writer knew her, knew she was married, knew she had kids, and, most significantly, stated that the writer knew Mary was having an affair with the school's superintendent. The letter went further, threatening Mary

that she had better finish the affair or there would be trouble. Written in block capitals, the letter read, "I know where you live. I've been observing your house and know you have children. This is no joke. Please take it serious[ly]."

Above: Mary Gillespie was the school bus driver, and kept her job throughout the scandal that the letters brought into her otherwise normal world.

THE THREATS CONTINUE

Mary did take it seriously, but told no one. A week later the mailman brought her another letter, again with the same tone and the same threats. Mary still said nothing, but she was concerned and kept an eye out for would-be stalkers. She would insist later that she was not having an affair but still, these letters were disconcerting, and they were about to get even worse.

One day soon after, Mary's husband, Ron, received a letter informing him of what was going on, saying that if he didn't stop it, he would die. Mary told Ron that it was nonsense. He believed her, but then another letter arrived. "Gillespie, you have had two weeks and done nothing. Make her admit the truth and inform the school board. If not, I will broadcast it on CBS, posters, signs, and billboards, until the truth comes out."

By now, Mary and Ron, the brunt of much Circleville gossip, were worried. Both had their suspicions, which they laid at the feet of their brother-in-law, Paul. Together they hatched a plan and sent similarly written letters to Paul's address, saying they knew he was the culprit and to stop. For a while it worked, but then, on an August day in 1977, the phone rang at Mary and Ron's home.

A MYSTERIOUS DEATH

Mary and her children never did find out who had made the call, but on hanging up the phone, Ron, visibly upset, told his children that he had had enough, he knew who their tormentor was, and he was going to confront him. Ominously, he took his pistol. Not long after, Ron Gillespie was found dead in his truck.

Below: Mary and Ron attempted to stop the sinister letters by writing copy-cat versions to their brother-in-law, who they thought was at the root of the letters.

On the face of it, Ron's death looked a straightforward accident. His truck had come off the road at a local intersection and struck a tree. Soon, though, Circleville residents were receiving letters stating that the police were covering up the truth, and strange facts started to emerge about the death. Ron's pistol, prior to his crash, had fired a single shot. Where or at whom, no one would ever know. No gunfire had been heard or reported.

It was also revealed that Ron's blood alcohol level had been one-and-a-half times the legal limit, news that shocked Ron's family and friends, who protested that he was by no means a heavy drinker. The cause of death—much to the letter writer's disappointment, who continued to argue the opposite—was deemed an accident.

Above: Ron Gillespie crashed his red Chevy into a tree, but the letter writer soon cast doubt over the accidental verdict of this crash.

ATTEMPTED MURDER

The town's letters—and Mary's problems—would not end there. Mary, her family members, and elected town officials all continued to receive letters of a cruel and lewd nature. Such was the pressure on Mary that she even admitted to now having an affair with the school superintendent, but she was adamant that this had started only after the letters so scarily suggested it. The town's eyes were starting to look toward Paul Freshour, Ron's brother-in-law, as the culprit, but he vociferously denied the accusations.

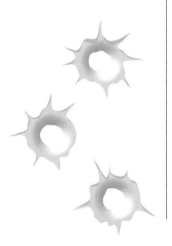

Above: Eventually, a crudely booby-trapped pistol led the police to a suspect, but one who continued to profess his innocence.

Events were about to take an even more sinister turn. Mary, who had, maybe surprisingly, kept her job, was one day driving the bus when she noticed a sign on a lamppost that threatened her daughter's life. Furious, she stopped the bus and took it down, but noticed a box with a string attached to it. She opened it and found a pistol inside it. This was a crude booby trap, designed to have gone off when opened. The police were called, as this case had become more than a set of nasty letters. The town sheriff, Dwight Radcliff, was now looking for a wannabe murderer.

The pistol's serial number had been scratched off with a file, but experts managed to trace it nonetheless, and found it belonged to Freshour. He maintained that it had been stolen, but the sheriff ordered a handwriting test and despite this being inconclusive, and the fact that the sighting of a man near the lamppost on which the booby trap was fixed was made at a time when Freshour had an alibi, Freshour was arrested and found guilty of attempted murder. He would plead his innocence, but for the town, justice had been done and the mystery of their letter writer had been solved.

Then the letters started to arrive once again. This wasn't enough to free Freshour from the 10 years he would serve behind bars, but it certainly continued the mystery. The letters arrived and were still post-marked from Columbus—Freshour's prison was in Lima—and often dated at times when he was in solitary confinement. Freshour died in 2012—the letters had stopped several years before—but the man who served a decade in prison remained adamant about his innocence.

— ALTERNATIVE — THEORIES

Much remains unexplained in this strange case. Paul Freshour was always quick to voice his innocence, arguing that his case had been badly investigated and that he was set up. It is a theory hard to argue with—Freshour himself received an anonymous letter while in prison that read, "Now when are you going to believe you aren't going to get out of there? I told you two years ago. When we set 'em up, they stay set up. Don't you listen at all?"

Also, Freshour was a model prisoner but when up for parole after seven years, it was denied, based on letters still being received, despite it being impossible for him to have sent them. Freshour and others pointed to the fact that the handwriting test used against him in court was inaccurate, as the sheriff had asked Freshour to try to replicate the handwriting; Freshour would argue that because he was innocent, he simply tried to do just that.

Above: Freshour had, unfortunately for him, done just what the sheriff asked, and excelled in his courtroom handwriting test.

The mystery remains. Some wonder about Mary's involvement, or that of the sheriff. When the television show *Unsolved Mysteries* showed an interest in the case just after Freshour's release, the producers received a letter. It read, "Forget Circleville, Ohio ... If you come to Ohio, you El sickos will pay. The Circleville Writer."

FURTHER READING

Clarke, Thurston. *The Last Campaign: Robert F. Kennedy and 82 Days That Inspired America*. New York: Henry Holt and Company, 2008.

Couttie, Bob. *Forbidden Knowledge: Paranormal Paradox*. Cambridge: Lutterworth Press, 1988.

DeLuca, Dan. *The Old Leather Man: Historical Accounts of a Connecticut and New York Legend*. Middletown: Wesleyan University Press, 2013.

Dunstan, Simon, and Gerrard Williams. *Grey Wolf: The Escape of Adolf Hitler*. New York: Sterling, 2013.

Jovanovic, Rob. *A Version of Reason: In Search of Richey Edwards*. London: Orion, 2010.

Kershaw, Ian. *Hitler*. London: Penguin, 2010.

Lunan, Duncan. *Children from the Sky*. London: Mutus Liber, 2012.

McCloskey, Keith. *Mountain of the Dead: The Dyatlov Pass Incident*. Stroud: The History Press, 2013.

Menzies, Gavin. *1421: The Year China Discovered the World*. London: Bantam Press, 2003.

Merrill, Alex. *Who Put Bella in the Wych Elm?* California: CreateSpace, 2018.

Mooney, Fraser. *Jerome: Solving the Mystery of Nova Scotia's Silent Castaway*. Halifax: Nimbus, 2008.

Nickell, Joe. *Looking for a Miracle: Weeping Icons, Relics, Stigmata, Visions and Healing Cures*. Amherst: Prometheus Books, 1999.

O'Callaghan, Sean. *The Informer: The Real Life Story of One Man's War Against Terrorism*. London: Corgi Press, 1999.

Oliver, Beverly, and Coke Buchanan. *Nightmare in Dallas*. Lancaster: Starburst Publications, 1994.

O'Sullivan, Shane. *Who Killed Bobby? The Unsolved Murder of Robert F. Kennedy*. New York: Skyhorse Publishing, 2018.

Owens, Paul. *The Baron of Rainbow Bridge: Overtoun's Death Leaping Dog Mystery Unravelled*. Edinburgh: Scarlet Quill Publishing, 2018.

Radford, Benjamin. *Tracking the Chupacabra: The Vampire Beast in Fact, Fiction, and Folklore*. Albuquerque: University of New Mexico Press, 2011.

Ramsden, Dave. *Unveiling the Mystic Cipher: Thomas Anson and the Shepherd's Monument*. California: CreateSpace, 2014.

Redfern, Nick. *Chupacabra Road Trip: In Search of the Elusive Beast*. Woodbury: Llewellyn Publications, 2015.

Regal, Brian, and Frank J. Esposito. *The Secret History of the Jersey Devil: How Quakers, Hucksters, and Benjamin Franklin Created a Monster*. Baltimore: John Hopkin University Press, 2018.

Simpson, Bland. *Ghost Ship of Diamond Shoals: The Mystery of the Carroll A. Deering*. Chapel Hill: University of North Carolina Press, 2005.

Waller, John. *A Time to Dance, A Time to Die: The Extraordinary Story of the Dancing Plague of 1518*. Thriplow: Icon Books, 2008.

INDEX

IMAGE CREDITS